Get Some Headspace

Get Some Headspace

Andy Puddicombe

HODDER &
STOUGHTON

First published in Great Britain in 2011 by Hodder & Stoughton
An Hachette UK company

1

A CIP catalogue record for this title is available from the British Library

Trade Paperback ISBN 978 1 444 72217 8
eBook ISBN 978 1 444 72223 9

Typeset in Celeste Regular by Palimpsest Book Production Limited, Falkirk, Stirlingshire

Printed and bound by Clays Ltd, St Ives plc

Hodder & Stoughton policy is to use papers that are natural, renewable and recyclable products and made from wood grown in sustainable forests. The logging and manufacturing processes are expected to conform to the environmental regulations of the country of origin.

Hodder & Stoughton Ltd
338 Euston Road
London NW1 3BH

www.hodder.co.uk

Acknowledgements

There are lots of people I'd like to thank for helping to make this project a reality, but first and foremost are the meditation masters who I've had the good fortune of studying with in monasteries and retreat centres around the world. Without the teachings from these remarkable individuals and the meditation traditions they embody, this book would have been impossible to write. I'd especially like to thank Donal Creedon for his guidance, kindness and invaluable friendship over the years.

I'd also like to thank my editor, Hannah Black, and the entire team at Hodder & Stoughton, for making this such an enjoyable process. Also to Antony Topping at Greene and Heaton, and Rich Pierson and Maria Schonfeld at Headspace, for casting a critical eye over so much unedited work and for all their helpful suggestions. And finally to Nick Begley for his valuable contribution to the scientific research sections of this book.

I'd like to add a special note of thanks to Ian Pierson, Misha Abramov and Marcus Cooper for their kind and generous support of the Headspace project. On behalf of all at Headspace, we simply can't thank you enough.

And last, but by no means least, I'd like to thank my family and friends for their enthusiastic support of this book and the entire Headspace project. In particular I'd like to thank my partner, Lucinda Insall-Jones, for her love, patience and unshakable faith in all that I do. It means the world to me.

Contents

Introduction

It was already well past midnight. I sat on top of the wall and looked down. The tall pine trees from inside the grounds gave me plenty of cover in the darkness, yet I couldn't resist the urge to look back one last time to see if I'd been followed. How had it come to this? I looked down again. It was just over 12 feet to the pavement. It may not sound that high but, crouching in a flimsy pair of sandals and my night clothes, the thought of jumping made me wince. What was I thinking wearing sandals? I'd tucked them into my trouser bottoms as I crept through the monastery, trying not to wake any of the other monks. I'd gone to the monastery to contemplate life, and yet here I was scaling its walls and contemplating my sandals as I prepared to jump back into the world.

It was never meant to be this way. I'd trained as a Buddhist monk before, and in much more challenging environments. But other monasteries had exuded a warmth, a kind and caring approach to what can only be described as a challenging, yet very fulfilling, way of life. This one had felt different though. It was a Buddhist monastery like no other. Locked in, day and night, surrounded by high stone walls and with no way of contacting anyone on the outside, at times it had felt more like a prison. I had no one to blame but myself of course, after all I'd gone there of my own free will. It's just that traditionally monasticism is a little different from the Mafia. It's not usually the case that once you become a monk, that's it, for life, with no way out. In fact on the contrary, Buddhist monasteries are known and respected for their tolerance and compassion. So how I'd ended up doing a bunk over a 12-foot wall to get away from one was a mystery really.

It had all started a few years earlier, when I made the decision to pack up and head off to Asia to become a monk. I was at university at the time, studying Sports Science. It may sound like a dramatic change in lifestyle, but it felt like one of the easiest decisions I'd ever made. Understandably, my friends and family were slightly more apprehensive than I was, perhaps wondering if I'd finally lost my mind, but all of them were none the less supportive. It was a different story at university, however. On hearing the news, my head of year suggested that a trip to see the doctor for some Prozac might be a more sensible option. As well meaning as he might have been, I couldn't help thinking he was missing the point. Did he really think I was going to find the type of happiness and fulfil-ment I was after in a bottle of prescription medicine? As I walked out the door of his office he said, 'Andy, you'll regret this decision for the rest of your life.' As it turns out, it happens to be one of the best decisions I've ever made.

Now you may be wondering what kind of person suddenly decides one day to head off to Asia and become a Buddhist monk. Perhaps you're imagining a 'self-medicating' student who'd lost his way, or a 'creative type' with the desire to rebel against a consumerist society. But the reality was actually far more mundane. At the time I just really struggled with my mind. Not in a straightjacket kind of way you understand, but I struggled with the endless thinking. It felt as if my mind was permanently switched on, going round and round like a washing machine. Some of the thoughts I liked. A lot of the thoughts I didn't like. The same was true of the emotions. As if a 'busy head' wasn't enough, I felt as though I was always drifting into unnecessary worry, frustration and sadness. They were quite ordinary levels of emotion, but they had a tendency to spin off out of control every now and then. And when they did, there was nothing I could do about it. It felt as though I was at the mercy of these feelings and would get blown around by them. On a good day, everything was fine. But on a bad day, it felt like my head would explode.

Given the strength of feeling, the desire to train the mind was never far from my thoughts. I had no idea how to do it properly, but I'd come into contact with meditation at a very early age and knew that it offered a potential solution. Now I wouldn't want you to think that I was some kind of child prodigy, and spent my teenage years sitting cross-legged on the floor, because that's most definitely not the case. I didn't take up the full-time study of meditation until I was twenty-two, but my first moment of headspace that I experienced at the age of eleven most definitely became a marker for what was possible. I'd love to say that it was a yearning to understand the meaning of life that motivated me to sign up for that first meditation class, but the truth is I went because I didn't want to feel left out. My parents had just separated and, looking for a way to cope, Mum had signed up for a six-week course. Seeing as my sister was going, I asked if I could go along too.

I guess I just got lucky the first time I tried it. I didn't have any expectations, so couldn't project any hopes or fears on the experience. Even at that age it's hard to ignore the change in the quality of mind that meditation can bring about. I'm not sure I'd ever experienced a quiet mind before then. I'd certainly never sat still in one place for such a long period of time. The problem of course was when I didn't get the same experience the next time I tried, or the time after that, I started to get very frustrated. In fact, it was as if the harder I tried to relax, the further I moved away from a place of relaxation. So this was how my meditation began, battling with my mind and getting increasingly frustrated.

When I look back now I'm not really all that surprised. The approach I was shown was a little 'far out', if you know what I mean. The language used was more 1960s than 1980s, and there were so many foreign words that I used to switch off in class. And then there was the constant reminder to 'just relax' and 'just let go'. Well, if I knew how to 'just relax' and 'just let go', then I wouldn't have been there in the first place. And as for sitting 30 or 40 minutes at a time, forget it.

This experience could well have put me off meditation for life. Support for the cause was certainly limited. My sister found it boring and gave up and, what with all her other commitments, Mum struggled to find the time. And as for support from friends, I can't imagine what I was thinking telling a couple of mates from school about it. By the time I walked into the classroom the next morning I was met by thirty students sitting cross-legged on their desks, eyes closed, chanting 'Om' through poorly stifled fits of laughter. Though I laugh about it now, at the time I was mortified. So from that point on I never mentioned it again to anyone, and eventually I gave it up. Besides, what with sport, girls and underage drinking arriving on the scene, it was difficult to imagine finding time for meditation.

You might think I was brought up in a way that somehow made meditation easier to accept as a concept. Maybe you're imagining me as an alternative character at school, walking around with bell-bottom flares, a pony-tail and smelling of incense. Or perhaps you have visions of my parents picking me up from school in a hemp-powered VW camper van with flowers painted down the side. I say this because I think it's easy to jump to conclusions, to tap into those stereotypes of meditation, and to think that it's only meant for a certain kind of person. But in reality, I think I was about as normal as you can be when you're a teenager.

I continued to dabble in meditation, until at the age of eighteen a crisis occurred, a series of tragic events that I'll come back to later, which eventually gave meditation an importance and relevance it had never had before. It's hard to deal with grief at any age. We're not trained for it, there's no formula for it, and most of us get by as best we can. For me that meant doing the only thing I knew how – pushing everything down inside, and hoping I would never have to deal with the feelings of loss and sadness that had so inconveniently arrived on my doorstep.

But like anything else in life, the more you push against something, the more tension you create. And eventually that tension has to find a way out. Fast-forward a couple of years, and I found myself studying at university. The first year flew by, and it was hard to imagine what more life had to offer. But then that tension, those feelings that had been ignored, time and time again, started to find their way to the surface. At first it was just uncomfortable, but before long it felt as though they were touching every single aspect of my life. Meeting with my head of year to give him the news that I had decided to leave and become a monk had been the least of my worries.

I had been brought up as a Christian, but by the time I reached my teens I felt no real connection with any particular religion. I'd read a few books over the years though, and a good friend of mine often used to speak about the philosophy and psychology of Buddhism. I guess it appealed in so much as it didn't really feel like a religion. And the stories of the meditation and the monks and nuns who had somehow mastered the mind sounded very attractive – not so much as a way of life, but in terms of the result.

When people ask me how I became a monk, the question is usually phrased something like, 'So, you just walk up the hill, knock on the door and ask to become a monk, do you?', and as ridiculous as that might sound, that's exactly what you do. But before you enthusiastically pack your bags, I should add that there's a little more to it than that, including a number of years of training as a lay-person, followed by full-time training as a novice monk and then, with your teacher's permission, you can become a fully ordained monk or nun.

In my impatience to find the right teacher, I moved often at first, from one monastery to the next, and from one country to the next. During that time I lived in India, Nepal, Thailand, Burma, Russia, Poland, Australia and Scotland, travelling across many other countries in the process, learning new techniques, each time building on the foundations of what I'd already learnt, and doing my best to integrate them into my life. With the exception of the walled fortress from which I was about to jump, I found everywhere I lived welcoming, friendly and thoroughly conducive to the training. And yes, thankfully, I eventually found the right teacher, or group of teachers as it turned out to be.

Living as a monk can be tricky – not everyone gets the whole 'bald-headed man in a skirt thing', and trying to demystify meditation for a secular audience while dressed as a monk, which is how I worked, can send out a very mixed message. It's one thing if you're living in a monastic community or retreat, where people around you understand the simplicity of a monk's robes, but when you're living in a city it's a little different. The more I spoke to people about the benefits of meditation, the more I found that many desperately wanted to find a way to relax, but were uncomfortable with the religious element that robes automatically imply. They simply wanted to find a way to cope with life, to deal with stress – in their work, their personal life, and in their own minds. They wanted to regain the sense of openness they remembered from childhood, that sense of appreciation in actually being alive. They weren't looking for spiritual enlightenment, nor were they needing therapy. They just wanted to know how to 'switch off' when they got home from work, how to fall asleep at night, how to improve their relationships, how to feel less anxious, sad or angry. People wanted to know how to control their cravings, to give up their addictions, to get a bit more perspective on life. But most of all they wanted to know how to deal with that nagging feeling that all was not quite as it should be, or could be – that feeling that there must be more to life than this. The integration of meditation into everyday life was key to my decision to stop being a monk and to live instead as a lay-person.

I became quite shy as a monk. Part of that was down to the intro-verted way of living, but an equally important factor was seeing more clearly the conditions of my own mind, which left me feeling a little exposed, a little naked, and this was something I was pretty keen to address. I was also keen to address the fact that I'd become very inactive. Prior to any monastic training I'd been incredibly physical and yet it was as though that had been put on hold for the best part of ten years. Talking to a friend one day, she mentioned that an old classmate of hers was training at the Moscow State Circus. As she knew I was a keen juggler and had done lots of gymnastics in the past, she thought this might be something worth checking out. Before long I was having private lessons and loving every bit of it. It was during one of these lessons that my teacher asked me if I knew anything about the degree in Circus Arts that was available in London. Yes, you read that right, a university degree in Circus Arts – seriously, you couldn't make it up! I began some tentative enquiries and, sure enough, it really did exist. The demand for places on the course is surprisingly high (let's be honest, who'd want to study atomic physics when you can swing around like a monkey on a trapeze all day long?), so on paper my chances didn't look good. But late one evening I received an e-mail to say that I'd been offered a conditional place – the condition being that I agreed to sign a disclaimer that, in no uncertain terms, said I was old, more likely to injure myself, and needed to take full responsibility for this fact. Old at thirty-two, who'd have thought it?

While the transition from monk to clown may not sound like the most obvious one, there are perhaps more similarities than first meet the eye. The application of moment-to-moment awareness into physical activity was to prove invaluable, in more ways than I could ever have imagined. Think of a circus act, whether it's juggling, tightrope, acrobatics or trapeze, all of them require the perfect balance of concentration and relaxation. Try too hard and you make a mistake. Don't try hard enough and you fall off or slip over.

One of the most challenging aspects of training at the circus was constantly being asked to step out of our comfort zones – for most of us on a daily basis. The ego takes quite a battering in that process and we were encouraged to take ourselves a little less seriously throughout. Funnily enough, this is very similar to the training in the monastery, where the ego is also being challenged. In clowning work-shops (still difficult to say with a straight face) we were encouraged to make fools of ourselves, to take risks, to try things out, confident in our ability to fail. We would be sent up on to the stage, with no material whatsoever, and be instructed what to do. And in those moments there was nothing but silence, nowhere to run. If we took too long to think about it, the teacher would simply bang a drum to indicate we were finished and send us off the stage. There was no room to escape in thought or reply in clever witticisms. It required a presence, a brutal honesty to put something out there and see what happens. Sometimes it was inspired and the thrill was exhilarating, other times it was painful and the result was humiliating. But somehow it didn't matter. What mattered was going out there and doing it, not thinking about it, not worrying what others might think, not even being attached to a particular result, just doing it.

Often in life we get so caught up in the analysis, the dissection of every possible outcome, that we miss an opportunity altogether. Of course, some things require careful consideration, but the more we live mindfully, in the moment, the more we start to get a sense of what feels right. Whether you think of it as a gut feeling, intuition, being guided, or just knowing for yourself that it's the right thing to do, this can be an incredibly liberating discovery.

The founding of Headspace

Teaching meditation was something I'd long felt passionately about, but I also felt a certain sense of duty to pass on the care and attention to detail that had been given to me by my own teachers. When I saw the way that meditation was sometimes being taught here in the UK, it amazed me that anyone could get any benefit from it at all. While the transition of meditation from East to West had been handled with great care and sensitivity by the monks and nuns of spiritual traditions, in the secular world it was done in the same way as we do everything else – in a hurry. It was as if we simply couldn't wait a moment longer to experience a quiet mind. So the techniques were extracted in isolation and without any context. This made them almost impossible to learn. How many people do you know who've tried meditation but then given it up? Worse still, how many people do you know who would never even give it a try because they think they'd be no good at it? But without knowing what meditation really is, without being given the essential instructions and guidance on how best to approach the techniques, how could it ever possibly work?

As you'll soon discover, the practise of meditation is about much more than simply sitting down for a set period of time each day.

Although it may be a key component, it is just one part of a broader system of mind training that incorporates three distinct aspects. Each aspect is equally important and, in order to get the most out of your meditation, the other two aspects also need to be learned. Traditionally, meditation students were taught first how to *approach* the technique, then how to *practise* it, before finally learning how to *integrate* the techniques into their everyday lives.

With the intention of presenting meditation as part of this broader system of mind training, Headspace officially launched in 2010. The idea was simple: to demystify meditation, to make it something accessible and relevant for modern-day living. Nothing kooky, nothing wacky, just straightforward tools that people could use to get some headspace. The idea was also to get as many people as possible to try meditation, not just to read about it, but to actually do it. There will undoubtedly come a time when sitting down to get some headspace for ten minutes a day is no more unusual than going out for a walk. Ten or fifteen years ago, it was hard to say the word Yoga without people sniggering, and yet going to the gym to take a yoga class is now no more strange than going there to do aerobics (in fact, arguably less so).

Although it took years of research, planning and development to make the project a reality, it is but a blink of the eye in terms of the history of the techniques. These are meditation exercises that have been passed down from teacher to student over thousands of years. That's more than enough time to refine and develop the techniques, not to mention iron out any creases. In a world of novelty, fads and fashions, there is something very reassuring about that authenticity. It was that authenticity which allowed me to start working alongside doctors, assisting in the adaptation of the techniques for medical use. It was the same authenticity that allowed me to start up in private practice as a Clinical Mindfulness Consultant, where over the years I've seen clients suffering from insomnia, impotence, and everything in-between.

So, there I was, perched on top of that wall. I took one final look behind me and jumped. I was sorry to leave the monastery in this way, but, looking back, I have no regrets about being there in the first place. Every monastery, retreat and meditation centre I have ever lived in or visited has taught me something. In fact, over the years I've had the privilege and good fortune to study with some incredible teachers, meditation masters in the truest sense of the word. If there's any wisdom to be found in these pages, then it's entirely down to them. The way I see it, my strongest qualification for writing this book is that along the way I've made just about every mistake possible in my meditation training, and so hopefully I can help you avoid making similar ones. This means giving you advice on how to best approach meditation, how best to practise meditation, and how best to integrate meditation into the rest of your life. Carrying a map is one thing, having someone to show you the way is quite another.

How to get the most from this book

Meditation is a wonderful skill with life-changing potential, but how you choose to use that skill is up to you. With increasing coverage of meditation and mindfulness in the media, many people seem to be in a hurry to define its purpose. But the truth is, *you* define the purpose by deciding how you choose to use it. When you learnt to ride a bike, I'm sure you were simply shown how to ride the bike, not how you should use that ability. Some use a bike to commute, for others it's to hang out with friends, and for a very few cycling may even become a career. But the skill of being able to remain in the saddle is the same for each. So while somebody else might have taught you how to ride, you define what cycling means to you, how you use it, and how it best suits your lifestyle. And so it is with the skill of meditation. It can be applied to any aspect of life and the value of it is equal only to the value you place upon it.

In order to get the best from this book, and consequently the many benefits of meditation, you don't need to choose just one area of your life that you'd like to focus on. At least not at first anyway. Meditation is much broader than that and the qualities that arise from it tend to inevitably impact those areas of life where it's needed most. However, it's useful to know how other people use meditation, to appreciate its full potential. For many it's the all-round stress buster, an aspirin for the mind. In short, a way of getting some headspace each day. For some, it's the foundation of a broader approach to mindfulness, an opportunity to touch base with what it means to be present and in the moment throughout the day. For others, it might be part of a personal development plan towards greater emotional stability, or integrated into a spiritual path of some kind. And then there are those who turn to meditation as a way of improving their relationships with partners, parents, children, friends, colleagues and associates.

Meditation is also used in much more specific ways. Ever since the UK National Institute for Clinical Excellence (NICE) approved the use of meditation (or mindfulness as it's known in the medical world), it's been used to treat a wide range of stress-related health symptoms. These include, but are no means limited to, chronic anxiety, depression, anger, addiction, compulsive behaviour, insomnia, muscle tension, sexual dysfunction and PMS.

Away from the medical world, but still with the intention of targeting one specific aspect of life, many people use meditation to give them an extra edge in a particular discipline, job, hobby or sport (the US Olympic team being a good example). And finally, stretching the boundaries of your imagination, meditation has even been adopted by the US marines to make them more focused and efficient on the front line.

Meditation and the mind

It may seem implausible that meditation could have such a broad range of benefits. But if you think about it, whatever you do that involves the mind is going to benefit from meditation. It's like fine-tuning the hard drive of a computer. And is there anything you do that *doesn't* involve the use of your mind? Given what a central role the mind plays in our lives, it's remarkable that this meditation revolution hasn't happened sooner. We don't think twice about exercising our bodies (well, most of the time anyway) and yet the wellbeing of the mind tends to take a back seat. Whether that's because nobody else can see it or because we think it's a lost cause is neither here nor there. The fact is, our entire existence is experienced through the mind. We depend on it for our sense of happiness and fulfilment in life and for positive relationships with others. So taking a few minutes out each day to train and maintain it is simply good common sense.

Meditation is an experience

As well as being a skill, meditation is also an experience. This means you need to *do* it in order to fully appreciate its value. Meditation is not just another fluffy concept, or philosophical idea; rather, it's a direct experience of the present moment. In the same way that it's up to you to define the *purpose* of meditation, it's also up to you to define the *experience* of meditation. Imagine a friend describing an amazing meal they'd eaten at a restaurant. Now imagine going there and eating it yourself. Hearing about the food and tasting the food are two completely different things, right? Or imagine reading a book about skydiving. No matter how much you reflect on the author's words and visualise yourself jumping from 10,000 feet, the experience will never come close to actually launching yourself out of a plane and hurtling towards the ground at 120 mph. So in order to *get* meditation, you need to *do* it.

I'm sure you know what it's like to buy a new book, become inspired, commit to changing your life and then, within a few days, be back in the same old habits wondering where it all went wrong. In the same way that sitting at home reading a diet book while eating chunky chocolate fudge ice-cream is never going to make you any thinner, simply *thinking* about what's written in this book is not going to give you any more headspace. Well, OK, it might give you a *little* more headspace, but the point is you need to actually *do* the exercises to experience the real benefit. And preferably not just once or twice either. Like going to the gym, it only works if you actually go and do the exercise on a regular basis. In fact, the real change will happen in those moments when you put the book down and practise the techniques. The change is subtle, intangible yet profound. It involves a growing sense of awareness and understanding that can't help but change the way you feel about both yourself and others.

But to really make the most of this book it's worth considering the possibility that not everything you've heard or read about meditation is necessarily true. In fact, some of the myths are spectacular. Unfortunately, many of the more popular misconceptions about meditation simply reinforce the same old patterns of thinking that most people would like to change. We're often rather attached to these ideas, and like old friends they feel familiar and comfortable to be around. But for genuine change to take place a certain amount of openness is required, a willingness to investigate. So this book isn't written to give you a definitive answer, to tell you what to believe and how to think. Nor is it written to solve all your problems and give you everlasting happiness. But it *is* a book that has the potential to fundamentally transform your experience of life if you put it to the test.

Meditation isn't about becoming a different person, a new person, or even a better person. It's about training in awareness and understanding how and why you think and feel the way you do, and getting a healthy sense of perspective in the process. It just so happens that when you do that, any changes you want to make in your life become that much more feasible. More than that, it shows you how to be OK with the way you are right now and how you feel. But put it to the test. Don't simply believe it works because that's what the scientists say. As valuable and fascinating as that research is, it will mean nothing if you don't directly experience the benefits yourself. So use the instructions, refer back to them, give it time, be patient, and see what 10 minutes a day can do for you.

The Headspace website

Although this book contains everything you need to know to get started with meditation, you'll find the Headspace website at www.getsomeheadspace.com to be an invaluable tool and companion. To download your audio-guided meditations and animations visit www.getsomeheadspace.com/headspace-book/get-some-headspace.

Audio downloads

Many find it easier to learn how to meditate when they are guided through the exercise by a teacher's voice. Make sure you visit www.getsomeheadspace.com/headspace-book/get-some-headspace to access the content for all the meditation and mindfulness techniques presented in this book. These downloads will give you the flexibility to meditate wherever you are. Readers can access exclusive audio downloads at www.getsomeheadspace.com/headspace-book/book1/hodder exclusivepodcasts. You'll be prompted to enter a simple password. Please remember not to listen to the audio downloads whilst driving.

The techniques

Throughout this book you'll find specific exercises designed to get you started and keep you going with your meditation practice. It may be a short two-minute exercise, introducing a particular aspect of meditation, or the full ten-minute version, known as Take10 in The Practice section. Or it might be a mindfulness exercise, designed to bring awareness to everyday activities such as eating, walking and exercise. There's even an exercise to help you get a good night's rest. But remember, it's when you put the book down and close your eyes to meditate that you'll feel the real benefit of these techniques.

The stories

Meditation instructions always used to be given in the form of a story and this is a tradition I've continued in writing this book. Stories make difficult concepts easy to grasp, and forgettable instructions easy to remember. Many of the stories presented here involve my own misunderstandings and struggles with meditation along the way. Sure, it would be easy to write about the times when I felt relaxed, calm and even blissful during meditation, and also about the radical, positive change that meditation has made to my life. But the real value is in looking back at the mistakes that I've made and sharing those with you, because that's where the learning took place and it's from those very same experiences that I can help you to get some headspace.

The science

In recent years the advancement of MRI technology, together with sophisticated brain-mapping software, has meant that neuroscientists are now able to observe the brain in a whole new way. This means that they've been able to discover exactly what happens to the brain when we're learning to meditate, and also some of the effects of long-term practice. At first it was assumed that it was simply the *activity* of the brain that changed during meditation, but multiple studies have shown that the structure of the brain itself can change, in a process known as neuroplasticity. So, in the same way that training the body can make a particular muscle thicker and stronger, so training the mind with meditation can make the area of the brain associated with happiness and wellbeing thicker and stronger.

For many people this new research can be motivating, inspiring and help to build confidence – especially in the early days of learning meditation. It's for this reason that I've included a handful of these research findings at the end of The Approach, The Practice and The Integration. They relate specifically to the information in those chapters, but have a much broader relevance too. But if you'd like to find out more about the research into meditation and mindfulness, then why not visit our dedicated research section of the website at: www.getsomeheadspace.com/Clinical-Research.

The case studies

In addition to the stories described above, you'll also find a chapter entitled Tales from the Clinic, which brings together a number of case studies from over the years. Some of these people have been referred to me by their doctor or GP for specific symptoms, but many more have come simply because they're looking for more headspace in their life. Written with the kind permission of each individual, these case studies demonstrate the simplicity, power and potential of a daily meditation practice.

Diary and feedback

Although meditation is all about letting go, keeping a diary when you're starting out can really make a difference. You can use the diary section provided at the back of this book to help keep track of your progress and visit our book page on the Headspace Facebook site to share your experiences, www.facebook.com/HeadspaceOfficial.

o

Mindfulness and meditation – what's the difference?

Let's be honest, it's hard to hear the word 'meditation' without thinking of a yogi in a loincloth on a mountain-top somewhere in the Himalayas. That, or a shaven-headed monk or nun sitting in a monastery, chanting, chiming bells and blowing horns, while cloaked in thick clouds of incense and orange robes (been there, done that). Or perhaps stoned-out hippies in tie-dye T-shirts spring to mind, or groups of New Age enthusiasts running around in the woods taking it in turns to hug a tree or two. There's no escaping it, the word 'meditation' comes with baggage.

When a few progressive Western doctors tried to introduce medi-tation into mainstream healthcare more than thirty years ago, they were pretty much laughed out of the hospital they worked in. Not to be deterred, they changed the name to 'mindfulness' and continued with their research. Now although mindfulness, in the form it has come to the West, has its origins in the Buddhist medi-tation tradition, there is nothing inherently 'Buddhist' about it. Mindfulness is the key ingredient of most meditation techniques and goes far beyond the formal aspect of sitting down with your eyes closed. Mindfulness means to be present, in the moment, undistracted. It implies resting the mind in its natural state of awareness, which is free of any bias or judgment. Sounds nice, doesn't it? This is in contrast to how most of us live our lives, which is to be constantly caught up with all the little (and big) thoughts and feelings, and to be critical and judgmental of ourselves and others.

It's usually when we're caught up in all the little things that we start to make mistakes. At least that's the way it's always been for me. And those mistakes can affect our performance at work, our relationships with others, even the bottom line in our bank account. Whenever I think about a lack of mindfulness I'm reminded of a time when I was living in Moscow. The school where I worked used to pay me in US dollars and as the salary was quite good I was able to save up a bit of money each month. It was just after the financial crisis of the late 1990s, and so nobody trusted the banks. People either hid their money under their mattress, or tried to find a way to squirrel it out of the country. I'd been saving up for a meditation retreat, so on my next flight back to the UK I decided to take what money I had with me.

The government had introduced strict rules about taking money out of the country – the main rule being that you *couldn't* take any. So I'd resorted to tucking $500 down the front of my underwear. Standing there in my monk's robes with a wad of cash shoved down my pants, I couldn't help but feel slightly guilty, no matter how good my intention was to spend it on a retreat. In fact, I got so caught up in all the little thoughts of anxiety, of rehearsing my Russian for the customs officials, that when I went to the toilet I completely forgot I'd put the money down there.

As it happens, the restroom was busy and so, with no urinals free, I went into one of the cubicles. I won't go into detail, but these toilets had seen better days and whoever had used it beforehand had forgotten to flush. I was still lost in thought and worry as I stood there and lifted up my robes. And then it happened. Before I could do anything, I watched in horror as $500 in loose notes fell into the pan. Needless to say, had I been more mindful and less caught up in all the thoughts, it would simply never have happened. I got distracted, and when you get distracted, you make mistakes. You may be wondering what happened next – did I really leave $500 floating in the toilet, or did I roll up my sleeves and do the unthinkable? Let's just say I ended up going on that retreat.

So mindfulness means to be present. It means being 'in the moment', experiencing life directly as it unfolds, rather than being distracted, caught up and lost in thought. It's not a contrived or temporary state of mind that you need to somehow create and maintain. On the contrary, it's a way of stepping back and resting the mind in its natural state, free from the usual chaos. Take a moment to imagine what it might be like to live life this way. Imagine how it would be to drop all the baggage, the stories, the arguments, the judgments and agendas that take up so much space in the mind. This is what it means to be mindful.

But after a lifetime of being lost in thought, the right kind of conditions are needed in order to learn how to step back in this way. That's where meditation comes in. There's nothing mystical about it. Meditation is simply a technique to provide you with the optimum conditions for practising the skill of mindfulness.

Of course you can experience being 'in the moment' or fully absorbed in the present with any activity, not just with the practice of meditation. In fact, you'll have no doubt experienced this feeling many times in your life before. Perhaps you were skiing down a mountain, riding a bike, listening to your favourite bit of music, playing with your child, or even watching a sunset. The problem with this approach is it tends to be a bit hit and miss and so we don't get to experience the feeling all that often. But by sitting down to meditate each day, even if it's for a very short time, that feeling of being present, aware, and in the moment, becomes increasingly familiar and is then that much easier to apply to the rest of your life. As with learning any new skill, if you want to get the very best out of it, you need to provide yourself with the very best conditions in which to learn. In fact the practice of meditation provides *such* good conditions for learning mindfulness that for many that's as far as they want to take it. Simply having ten minutes of resting the mind each day can feel enough.

The idea of mindfulness and meditation and how they relate is not necessarily that easy to grasp. So try thinking of it this way: imagine you're learning to drive a car, presumably you'd head out to a quiet country road rather than a busy motorway at first. Of course you can drive on either, but one is much easier than the other when you're learning. The same is true of mindfulness. You can use it in any situation and for any purpose, but the easiest place to learn the skill of mindfulness is during meditation. The funny thing is, even when you feel confident in applying mindfulness to everyday life, you'll probably still want to take a short time out to meditate each day. That's because no matter how good a driver you might be, there's something comforting, and even exhilarating, about driving along a quiet country road that a motorway never can quite match. What's more, it also gives you the time and space to notice what's going on around you, to admire the scenery.

The distinction between meditation and mindfulness may not sound that important, and often the words are used interchangeably. But unless you're about to pack your bags and start life afresh as a monk or a nun, this distinction matters a lot. Because so long as you're living life outside of a mountain retreat, there'll always be a limited amount of time to sit down and practise meditation in a formal, structured way. Often I hear people saying 'I don't have time to meditate, I'm too busy, I've got too much to do, I'm too stressed!' But if we look at the broader context, in terms of training and cultivating the mind no matter where we are or what we're doing, then suddenly it starts to look more achievable. At the very least it sounds more compatible with all the responsibilities and commitments of modern-day living. And that's what will hopefully make this book such an invaluable guide for you. It will show you how you can continue to live in the world with a daily meditation practice bite-sized enough to fit into your schedule, yet long enough to make a difference. It will also show you how you can use this broader idea of 'mind training' or 'mindfulness' to transform your experience of everyday life.

I'm sure there'll be some seasoned meditators who'll throw their hands up in horror at the idea of a ten-minute meditation. If you're one of them, then at first glance I appreciate this may sound like the equivalent of a ready-cooked-microwavable meal. But examine the intentions of mind training a little more closely, and you'll see that the idea of 'little and often' makes a great deal of sense. We need to be flexible, adaptive and responsive in our approach to meditation. It's all well and good to sit perfectly still for an hour, but if you're unable to maintain your awareness for all that time, then little benefit will come from it. And what about the other twenty-three hours of the day? Like so many things in life, when it comes to meditation it's about quality rather than quantity. Start by taking just ten minutes. If you find it easy, want to do more and have the time, then great. But there are still many benefits to be had from simply sitting for ten minutes a day. Even if I ignore all the anecdotal benefits that I've heard and seen over the years, there's now substantial scientific evidence (which you'll notice throughout the book) to support the health benefits of short, regular, daily meditation sessions.

What is headspace?

If mindfulness is the ability to be present, to rest in the moment whatever you're doing, and meditation is the best way of learning that skill, then 'headspace' could be considered the outcome. I'm using the word in the broadest possible context here. In fact, many people might choose to use the word 'happiness' instead. The problem with the word 'happiness' is it tends to get confused with the *emotion* of happiness. Don't get me wrong, having fun, enjoying yourself, laughing and smiling are wonderful aspects of life. Who wouldn't want to experience more of these things? But life's not continually like that. Stuff happens. And that 'stuff' is not always nice. As much as we try to ignore the fact, life can be difficult, stressful, upsetting and even painful at times. So the type of happiness that just comes and goes dependent on our circumstances and mood is too temporary, too unstable, to offer us any lasting sense of calm or clarity.

That's why I prefer the word 'headspace'. It describes an underlying sense of peace, a feeling of fulfilment or unshakeable contentment, no matter what emotion might be in play at that time. Headspace is not a quality of mind dependent on surface emotions; this means it can be experienced just as clearly in periods of sadness or anger as it can in times of excitement and laughter. Essentially it's 'being OK' with whatever thoughts you're experiencing or emotions you're feeling. That's why meditation feels so good, often even the very first time. It doesn't (necessarily) leave you rolling around in laughter or swinging from the chandeliers, but it leaves you with the sense of having touched upon that underlying sense of contentment, that place where you just know that everything is OK. The consequences of this can be life changing.

This distinction between headspace and the emotion of happiness is an important one. For some reason we've come to believe that happiness should be the default setting in life and, therefore, anything different is somehow wrong. Based on this assumption we tend to resist the source of unhappiness – physically, mentally and emotionally. It's usually at this stage that things get complicated. Life can begin to feel like a chore, and an endless struggle to chase and maintain that feeling of happiness. We get hooked on the temporary rush or pleasure of a new experience, whatever that is, and then need to feed it the whole time. It doesn't matter whether we feed it with food, drink, drugs, clothes, cars, relationships, work, or even the peace and quiet of the countryside. If we become dependent on it for our happiness, then we're trapped. What happens when we can't have it any more? And what happens when the excitement wears off?

For many, their entire life revolves around this pursuit of happiness. Yet how many people do you know who are truly happy? And by that I mean, how many people do you know who have that unshakeable sense of underlying headspace? Has this approach of chasing one thing after the next worked for you in terms of giving you headspace? It's as if we rush around creating all this mental chatter in our pursuit of *temporary* happiness, without realising that all the noise is simply drowning out the natural headspace that is already there, just waiting to be acknowledged.

During my travels in India I met with a man called Joshi. He was one of those people who is instantly likeable. He started talking to me as I was waiting for a bus one day. As anyone who's been to India will tell you, that can be a long wait, especially in the mountains. We got on well and had a few mutual interests – the most notable being meditation. Over the next few weeks we spent more time talking and sharing our experiences. Each day Joshi weaved into the conversation just a little bit more about his life.

A few years before we met, Joshi had lived with his wife and four children. Because neither his parents or in-laws were particularly wealthy, they also lived with the family. Joshi said that although it had been a very crowded house back then, it had also been a very happy one. But not long after his wife had returned to work, having had their fourth baby, she was tragically killed in a road accident. Her parents and her newborn child were with her in the car at the time. It was a very serious accident and there were no survivors. As I think back to Joshi telling me this story, it still brings tears to my eyes. He said that the pain had been unbearable, that he hadn't been able to face the world, that all he wanted to do was to retreat within himself and hide away at home. But his parents reminded him that he still had three children who needed his care and support, and that what they needed most of all was a father who was there for them. So Joshi threw himself into looking after the children and giving them his undivided attention whenever he could.

A few months later the monsoon arrived and with it came the typical floods in that region of the country. As a result there was a lot of standing water in the area and the incidence of disease shot up dramatically. Along with many other children in the village, Joshi's children got very ill. His mother also became unwell. Within two weeks, all three children and his mother had died. His mother had been weak beforehand and passed away quickly. The children had been stronger, but not so strong that they could fight off the illness. Within three short months this one man had lost his wife, his mother, his children, and his in-laws. His father was the only survivor in his entire family. Unable to live in the same house that had witnessed so much tragedy, Joshi went to stay with his friends. His father, unable to leave the house that he had always called home, remained to look after it. Within just a few days of moving, Joshi received the news that his house had burnt down, with his father seemingly trapped inside. Joshi said he still wasn't sure whether it had been an accident or whether his father had decided that he was simply unable to go on.

As I heard this story unfold I felt increasingly ashamed of my grumbling, moaning and complaining in life – of always wanting things to be exactly as I wanted them to be, and not being satisfied unless I got my way. How could I get so upset about the train being late, or being woken up in the middle of the night, or a disagreement with a friend? Here was a man who had suffered in a way that I could only ever imagine, and yet who still seemed to have this extraordinary sense of calm and presence about him. I asked him what he'd done since losing his family and he described how he'd moved to this new area. He said that having no family, no home and no money had forced him to think very differently about life. In the end he'd chosen to live in a meditation centre, where he spent most of his time. I asked whether he thought that his time spent meditating had changed the way he felt about what had happened. He replied that it hadn't changed the way he felt, but had instead changed his experience of those feelings. He said that while he still felt a great sense of loss and sadness at times, he perceived it differently. He described how he'd found a place beneath those thoughts and feelings where there was a sense of peace, of stillness and of calm. He said that it was the one thing that could never be taken away from him, that no matter what else happened to him in life, he would always have this place within himself to return to.

While this may be an extreme example, life will inevitably serve up challenges for all of us, situations we wish were different or would prefer to be otherwise (although hopefully none so tragic as the story of Joshi). Meditation can't change that, nor can anything else for that matter. It's part of being human, of living in this world. Sometimes there'll be external situations that *require* change, that might even *demand* change, and you'll need to handle these situations skilfully, with mindfulness. But when it comes to the way you think and feel about those situations, the starting point is to acknowledge that it's the mind itself that defines your experience. This is why training the mind is so important. By changing the way in which you *see* the world, you effectively *change* the world around you.

I think often this point is misunderstood and people feel as though they have to give up their dreams and ambitions in life in order to practise meditation. But that's not the case at all. There is something inherently human about striving to achieve something, and having a sense of purpose and direction in life is vital. But, if anything, meditation can be used to clarify and support that purpose, because what the practice will show you, in a very direct way, is that a lasting sense of happiness and sense of headspace is not dependent on these things. This will allow you to live with a greater sense of freedom and ease, confident in where you're heading in life and yet not so attached to the outcome that an unexpected obstacle or unfavourable outcome will result in heartbreak and loss. It is a subtle yet profound shift in perspective.

The need for headspace

When was the last time you sat down, completely still, undistracted and undisturbed, with no television, music, books, magazines, food, drink, telephone, computer, friends, family, or something you needed to think about or resolve in your own mind? If you've never looked at anything like meditation before, then my guess is probably never. Because usually, even if we're just lying in bed, we still tend to be involved in the thought process. So for many people, the idea of doing absolutely nothing sounds at best boring and at worst positively frightening. In fact, we're so busy doing stuff the whole time that we no longer have any reference point for what it means to be still, simply resting the mind. We've become addicted to 'doing stuff', even if it's just thinking. So it's not surprising that sitting still without distractions can feel a little alien at first.

Exercise 1: not doing

Try it now. Without moving from where you're sitting, just close the book and place it in your lap. You don't need to sit in any particular way, but just gently close your eyes and sit for a minute or two. It's no problem if lots of thoughts pop up, you can let them come and go for now, but see what it feels like to sit still, not doing anything, for just a minute or two.

How was it? Perhaps it felt very relaxing to do nothing. Or perhaps you felt the need to 'do' something, even if it was doing something within the exercise itself. Maybe you felt the urge to focus on something, to keep yourself occupied in some way. Don't worry, it's not a test, and there'll be plenty to keep you occupied when we get on to the meditation in the next section. But I think there's something beneficial, even at this early stage, in noticing the habit or desire to *do* something the whole time. If you *didn't* experience the urge to do something, then you might like to try the exercise again, but this time for a few minutes longer.

Now I'm not suggesting that there's anything wrong with watching television, listening to music, having a drink, going shopping or hanging out with friends. On the contrary, these are all things to be enjoyed. It's just useful to recognise that they facilitate a certain amount of *temporary* happiness, rather than a lasting sense of headspace. Have you ever finished work for the day feeling really strung out with a busy mind? Perhaps you decided to just 'switch off' for the evening and watch a bit of television to make yourself feel better. If the programme was really good and you were fully distracted, then it might have felt as though it gave you a break from all those thoughts. But if it was not very interesting, or had lots of adverts, it will probably have created just enough space for those thoughts to arise every now and then. Either way, when the programme finished, there's a pretty good chance that all those thoughts and feelings will have flooded back again. Sure, they may not have come back with the same intensity, but they are likely to have been there in the background none the less.

And this is how most people live their lives, moving from one distraction to the next. When they're at work they're too busy, too distracted, to be aware of how they really feel, so when they get home they're suddenly confronted by lots of thoughts. If they manage to keep themselves occupied during the evening, then they may not even become aware of these thoughts until they go to bed at night. You know how it goes, you put your head on the pillow and it appears as though the mind suddenly goes into overdrive. Of course, the thoughts have been there all along, it's just that without any distractions you become aware of them. Or it can be the other way around. Some people have such busy social lives or family lives that it's not until they get to work that they become aware of just how frazzled they feel, of all the thoughts racing around in the mind.

All these distractions affect our ability to concentrate, perform and live at anywhere near our optimum level. Needless to say, if the mind is always racing from one thought to the next, then our ability to focus will be seriously impaired.

Exercise 2: the senses

Take another two minutes to do this short exercise. As before, stay sitting exactly as you are right now. After putting the book down in your lap, gently focus on one of the physical senses, preferably sound or sight at this stage. I'd recommend using background sounds and closing your eyes, but as sounds can be a little unpredictable at times, you might prefer to keep your eyes open and gaze at a particular object in the room instead, or perhaps a point on the wall. Whichever sense you choose, try focusing on it for as long as possible, but in a very light and easy way. If you get distracted by thoughts or other physical senses, simply bring your attention back to the object of focus and continue as before.

How did you find it? Were you able to focus on it quite easily, or did you find your mind kept wandering off with other thoughts? How long did it take before you got distracted? Maybe you found you were able to maintain a vague sense of awareness but were thinking about other things at the same time. As unlikely as it may sound, for many people focusing on an object for even one minute is quite an achievement. When you think how long you need to focus on your work, or looking after your family, perhaps listening to a friend, or even driving a car, only being able to focus for such a short period of time can be quite a worry.

Hostage to technology

As if we didn't already have enough ways of avoiding what's going on in our minds, we now have e-mails and social media routed to our mobiles so we can be *truly* distracted all day. As convenient as that may be, it means that now even the slightest feeling of boredom or restlessness is a trigger to get online and keep busy. Take a moment to think about it. What's the first thing you do each day? Is it checking your e-mails? Perhaps sending messages on Facebook, interacting with friends or work colleagues through Twitter? And what's the last thing you do at night before going to sleep? If the research is accurate, then there's a pretty good chance that you'll be doing at least one of these things at either end of the day, if not all of them. It's pretty hard to switch off when you're permanently plugged in.

I read a story in the newspaper about a man who'd become so addicted to technology, so terrified that he might miss something important or perhaps offend someone by not replying to them, that he'd taken to sleeping with his smartphone on his chest. Not only that, but he also took his laptop to bed with him and slept with it by his side – actually *in* the bed. This is a married man (at least at the time of writing) who shares the bed with his wife. The irony is that he had such a flood of electronic data flowing into his life, that despite taking his computer to bed, he still managed to somehow miss an e-mail in which he was offered $1.3 million for his company that he'd put up for sale. This may be an extreme example, but pretty much everyone I know complains of feeling overwhelmed by the amount of electronic data in their life. When I was living as a monk I used to think 'well just turn it off, don't use it'. But living out in the world and having now to embrace all these things in my own work, I can see that it's not as simple as just turning it off or ignoring it. So instead of trying to stop or change it, we need to look at how we can relate to it skilfully and not feel overwhelmed.

Fundamental principles of training the mind

That idea brings us back to the fundamental principles of training the mind. Mindfulness doesn't require you to change anything. In becoming increasingly aware of your own mind you may find you choose to make some changes in your external life, but that's entirely up to you. There's no need to give everything up, or radically change your lifestyle in any way. Dramatic changes like this are rarely sustainable, which is what makes a mindful way of living so achievable. You can keep living as you always have done, if that's what you want to do. Mindfulness is about learning how to change your *experience* of that lifestyle. It's about finding a way to live as you are, but with an underlying sense of fulfilment. And then, if you feel as though you want to make some changes, then of course feel free. The difference is, any changes you make will be sustainable.

Stress

The consequence of living such a busy life, with so many responsibilities and choices, is that our bodies and minds are constantly working overtime. Many people I know say that even when they're asleep at night it feels as though the cogs just keep on turning. So it's no coincidence that the rate of stress-related illness has increased at the same time as our lives have become more complicated. According to the UK National Office of Statistics, the prevalence of anxiety, depression, irritability, addiction and compulsive behaviour have all risen sharply in recent years, accompanied by all the usual physical symptoms of stress such as fatigue, hypertension and insomnia.

People come to the clinic where I work for all kinds of different reasons, but the symptoms of stress are by far the most common. Sometimes people come along without prompting, at other times they may get a nudge from their partner, family member or friend. Occasionally the symptoms are so bad that their doctor refers them. But mostly these are ordinary people looking to find a way to cope a bit better in life. Perhaps they feel under pressure at work, overwhelmed by family life, tired of obsessive thinking or consistently acting in a way that is causing themselves or others harm. Most of them are simply looking for a little more headspace in their lives. In fact, at the end of the book you'll find case studies for some of these individuals, who've generously agreed to share their experiences.

Stress can make us do all kinds of funny things. It can lead to us saying things we wish we hadn't, doing things we wish we hadn't. It affects the way we feel about ourselves and the way in which we interact with others. Of course, a certain kind of stress or challenge can leave us feeling fulfilled, having achieved an objective. But too often it tends to spill over into the other (not so useful) kind of stress, and we are left wondering what life is about. This is where the importance of training the mind, of maintaining contact with this underlying sense of fulfilment and happiness no matter what's happening in our lives, can make such a profound difference. This is what it means to have headspace.

Relationships

Mindfulness will undoubtedly help you get some headspace and make a difference to your life. That's probably why you are reading this book in the first place. But there's another good reason for training in mindfulness. Because, whether we like it or not, we share the world in which we live with other people and, unless we want to live as a solitary yogi or hermit in the mountains, we're always going to have to interact with others. So who benefits most from your increased sense of headspace? Is it you, or is it the people around you? It's safe to assume that if you're in a better place because you're practising mindfulness and doing your meditation each day, then you're going to interact with others in a more positive way as well.

This is perhaps the most neglected aspect of mind training. When meditation came from the East to the West, for some reason it quickly became about 'me, myself and I'. While this was perhaps inevitable at first, it's important that we now, as time goes by, have the intention to make it a more altruistic type of training. My guess is that you probably struggle most in life when you are focusing on your own problems, because that's what we tend to do as humans. We like to obsess, ruminate and analyse endlessly. OK, so we don't actually *like* doing it, but it can sometimes feel impossible to stop it. But what happens when you think about someone else's problems instead? The nature of the internal struggle changes, right? Sure, you might feel sad or upset when you think about their difficulties, but it feels very different to obsessing about your own problems. There's a shift in persepective. And this is such an important part of training the mind. By focusing less on your own worries and more on the potential happiness of others you actually create more headspace for yourself. Not only that, but the mind becomes softer, more malleable, easier to work with. It tends to be quicker to settle on the object of meditation, less easily distracted by passing thoughts. It also tends to be clearer, more stable and less reactive to volatile emotions. So giving your practice an altruistic edge is about so much more than simply doing the right thing.

It should come as no surprise that the impact this simple skill can have on your relationships with others is quite profound. In becoming more aware of every*thing* and every*one*, you inevitably become more aware of others. You start to notice how sometimes you might unintentionally (or even intentionally) push their buttons, or notice what causes them to push yours. You start to listen to what they're actually saying, rather than thinking about what you'd like them to say or what you're going to say next. And when these things begin to happen you'll notice that your relationships with others really start to change. But so long as we're immersed in our own thoughts the whole time, it's very difficult to truly find time for others.

The three components of mind training

Traditionally, meditation was never practised alone. It was always part of a broader system of mind training. More specifically, meditation was just one part of three key aspects. The first part of the training would be understanding how to *approach* the technique. This means discovering the dynamics of the mind and how it's likely to behave when you *practise* the technique. Only then would you be introduced to the actual meditation techniques. But there was a third aspect too. Having gained a sense of familiarity with the technique, the emphasis would be on the *integration* of that quality of mind into everyday life. In the rush to bring meditation to the West, two of these aspects have been largely neglected. And without those two pieces of the jigsaw puzzle, the essence of meditation is lost. It becomes something isolated from its original context and therefore less effective. It also has considerably less impact on your everyday life. So perhaps it's no surprise that people have struggled so much with meditation over the years. For meditation to really work, to get the very best from the techniques, it's vital that all three components are present: how best to approach the techniques, how best to practise the techniques, and how best to integrate the techniques.

No one aspect of this jigsaw is more, or less, important than the next. Imagine you're given a beautiful classic car to look after. Now you've never driven a car before, never had any lessons, and the car is so unusual, so rare, that you're not even too sure what all the different pedals, levers and buttons do. The approach to meditation is like learning how to drive the car. You don't need to understand all the mechanics under the bonnet, but you need to know how to operate the various pedals, levers and buttons. You'll also need to get used to the power of the car, your positioning on the road, and of course to the unpredictability of all the other cars around you. This is the *approach*.

But this is no ordinary car, it's a classic car, and so it requires that
the engine is turned over on a regular basis in order for it to remain
healthy, and for it to work at its optimum capacity next time you
want to take it for a drive. If you're not familiar with classic cars
then this might sound a little strange, but it's just what these old
engines need once in a while. That's where the meditation comes in,
sitting down each day and without actually taking the car for a ride,
you sit there and allow the engine to tick over at its own comfortable pace while you listen to it chugging away, becoming more
familiar with how it sounds and how it feels. This is the *practice*.

But then what good is a car if you never take it anywhere? And
it's the same with meditation. The purpose of learning meditation
is not so that you can spend your life sitting on your backside with
your eyes closed, but to integrate that familiarity of awareness into
other areas of your life. This is the *integration*.

This means there are two different ways of using meditation. One
is the 'aspirin' approach, as I like to call it. We go out, lead busy
lives, get stressed, need something to make us feel better afterwards, and so do some meditation. Feeling better, refreshed, we
then go out again, lead busy lives again, get stressed again, until
we once more need something to make us feel better. There's
nothing wrong with this approach – in fact, you may well get considerable headspace from it, but it's limited when compared to the
second approach, which works to integrate that same quality of
mind into the remainder of your life.

The amount of time most people are able to dedicate towards the
practice of seated meditation is but a fraction of the day. The great
thing about applying mindfulness to the rest of the day is that it
doesn't require you to take any more time out, or to change your
schedule in some way. In fact, you can just keep on doing exactly
what you had planned. The difference is not in the activity, but the
way in which you direct your mind while doing those things.

The Approach

Meditation and thoughts

When I set off for my very first monastery, I was convinced that meditation was all about stopping thoughts. I'd heard about this 'quiet empty mind', which could supposedly be achieved through meditation, and I was desperate to taste it. Sure, I'd had a glimpse or two over the years, but I imagined it as something never-ending, a bubble in which there was nothing but space, and through which nothing unpleasant could enter. I imagined it as a place that was free from thoughts and feelings. I'm not sure how I ever imagined it was possible to live without thoughts or feelings, but this is how I approached meditation from the beginning. But trying to create this bubble, to achieve this state of mind which I'd assumed I needed to reach to be meditating 'properly', is probably one of the most common misconceptions about meditation.

I received some excellent instruction during this time, but the style in which it was delivered only served to reinforce many of the erroneous ideas I had about it. Each day I'd visit the teacher and explain how my meditation was going, and how there were all these thoughts racing through my mind that I couldn't stop no matter what I tried. And each day he'd tell me to be more vigilant, to try harder to catch the thoughts the moment they arose in the mind. In no time I became a nervous wreck. I'd sit 'on guard' hour after hour. It felt like the mental equivalent of the 'whack-a-mole' game you find in a fairground, constantly waiting for the next thought to arrive so that I could jump on it and extinguish it.

With eighteen hours of meditation every day and just three hours or so for sleep, it wasn't long before I'd exhausted myself completely. I'd sit there in the temple straining to achieve something. Anything. But with every extra ounce of effort I moved further away from that which I was seeking. The other monks from the local area looked perfectly relaxed. In fact, there were a few who seemed to regularly nod off. Now while that's obviously not the purpose of meditation, when you're forcing it as much as I was, the idea of sleep was positively dreamy.

After a little while my teacher realised that I was putting in too much effort and instructed me to try less. But by this stage I was putting too much effort into everything. Even into trying less. This struggle went on for some time until I was fortunate enough to meet a teacher who seemed to have a natural gift for story-telling, for explaining things in a way I could easily understand. What he said to me came as quite a shock, because his description of medi-tation was radically different to what I'd imagined.

The road

He began by asking me to imagine I was sitting on the side of a very busy road, with a blindfold around my head. 'Now,' he said, 'maybe you can hear the background noise, the cars whizzing by, but you can't see them because you have your eyes covered, right?' I imagined myself sitting on the grass verge of a motorway (the

M4 as it happens) and nodded in agreement. 'So,' he went on, 'before you start to meditate it can feel a bit like this. Because of all the background noise in the mind, all the thoughts, it means that even when you sit down to relax or go to bed at night, it still feels as though this noise continues, yes?' It was hard to argue with this, because it did indeed feel as though there was always a certain amount of background noise or restlessness in my mind, even when I was not consciously aware of the individual thoughts.

'Now, imagine taking the blindfold off,' he continued, 'For the first time you see the road, your mind, clearly. You see the cars racing by, the different colours, shapes and sizes. Maybe sometimes you are attracted by the sound of the cars, at other times more interested in their appearance. But this is what it's like when you first take off the blindfold.' He started laughing to himself. 'You know,' he said, 'sometimes it's at this point that people learning meditation say some very funny things. They start to blame their thoughts and feelings on the meditation. Can you believe it?' he asked mockingly. 'They come and see me and say "I don't know what's happening, where all these thoughts are coming from. I never usually think this much, it must be the meditation making me think all the time", as if the meditation is somehow making their situation worse.' His laughter trailed off as he picked up the thread of his explanation.

'So, the first thing to get straight is that meditation does not make you think! All it does is shine a big bright light on your mind so that you can see it more clearly. This bright light is awareness. You may not like what you see when you switch the light on, but it's a clear and accurate reflection of how your mind behaves on a daily basis.' I sat there and considered his words. He was definitely right about one thing – I'd been blaming meditation for the state of my mind ever since I started. I couldn't believe that my mind was really like that all the time. Or at least I didn't want to believe it was. I wondered if perhaps I was beyond help altogether, that no amount of meditation was going to help. It turns out that this is a surprisingly common feeling though, so be reassured if you feel this way too.

My teacher seemed to sense where I was going and interrupted my thoughts. 'This is how the mind looks to begin with,' he said softly, 'not just your mind, but everybody's. That's why training the mind is so important. When you see the mind in this confused state it's very difficult to know what to do about it. For some people it's difficult not to panic. Sometimes people try to stop the thoughts through force. At other times they try and ignore them, to think about something else instead. Or if the thoughts are very interesting, then they might try to encourage them and get involved in them. But all these tactics are just ways of trying to avoid the reality of what is. If you think back to the busy road, it's no different from getting up from the side of the road, running among the cars and trying to control the traffic.' He paused for a moment. 'This is quite a risky strategy,' he said, laughing again.

Sound familiar? Once again, he was right. That's exactly what I'd been doing and not just in my meditation. It summed up my life in general. I'd been trying to control everything. Seeing the chaos of my mind when I sat to meditate had simply triggered the habitual tendency to jump in and take charge, to sort everything out. When that hadn't worked, I'd just ramped up the effort. But then that's what we're taught when we're young, isn't it? 'Must try harder.' So I'd just kept trying harder. But it turns out no amount of force will result in a feeling of calm.

My teacher continued by making a suggestion. 'Here's an idea – rather than running around in the traffic trying to control everything, why not try staying where you are for a moment? What happens then? What happens when you stay on the side of the road and just watch as the traffic goes past? Maybe it's rush hour and the road's full of cars, or maybe it's the middle of the night and there are very few cars at all. It doesn't really matter which it is. The point is to get used to "holding your seat" on the side of the road and watching the traffic go by.' I found the idea of just watching the thoughts go by quite easy to imagine and for once I was actually in a hurry to get back to my meditation cushion.

'When you start to approach your meditation in this way you'll notice that your perspective changes,' he said. 'In stepping back from the thoughts and feelings, there will be a sense of increased space. It might feel as if you are simply an observer, watching the thoughts, the traffic, go by. Sometimes you might forget,' he said, smiling knowingly, 'and before you know it you'll find yourself running down the road after a fancy-looking car. This is what happens when you experience a pleasant thought. You see it, get caught up in it, and end up chasing after the thought.' He was now laughing loudly as he imagined me chasing the cars. 'But then all of a sudden, you'll realise what you're doing and, *in that moment*, you'll have the opportunity to return to your seat at the side of the road. At other times, you might see some traffic coming that you don't like the look of. Maybe it's an old rusty car, an unpleasant thought, and you'll no doubt rush out into the traffic to try and stop it. You might try to resist this feeling or thought for quite some time before you realise that you're back in the road again. But the moment you do, *in that moment*, you have the opportunity to take up your position on the side of the road again.' He continued, now speaking more deliberately. 'Over time, this will get easier. You won't want to run out into the road quite so often and you'll find it easier and easier to just sit and watch the thoughts go by. *This* is the process of meditation.'

It's worth taking some time to reflect on this analogy and as I sat there I considered what he'd said. It all made so much sense, at least theoretically. But there were a couple of points that didn't feel right. If I was just sitting there as an observer to the thoughts, then who was doing the thinking? Surely I can't be doing both at the same time? 'Your thoughts are autonomous,' he explained. 'Of course, if you want to think about something you can, you have that ability to reflect, to remember, or to project into the future and imagine how things might be. But what about the thoughts that just "pop" into your mind when you sit to meditate, or when you're walking down the street, or sitting at your desk trying to read a book? What about those thoughts? You didn't bring those thoughts to mind, did you? They *came* to mind. One minute you're reading a book and the next the thought of an old friend "pops" into your mind. You haven't thought of this friend for a long time and you made no conscious effort to *bring* him to mind and yet, all of a sudden, there he is!' This was definitely something I'd experienced a lot. I don't know if it's something that ever happens to you, but I'd often start reading a page of a book, only to reach the end and realise that not a word had gone in. Inevitably, somewhere along the way a thought had popped up and I'd become distracted, often without even being aware of it.

'So,' he continued, 'these thoughts that we try so hard to suppress, to get away from or to stop altogether, are pretty much just popping up whenever they feel like it, right? We like to think we control our minds, control the flow of thought, but if it was possible to do that then you wouldn't have travelled halfway around the world for my advice.' He pointed at me, playfully, laughing. 'In fact, if it were possible to control your thoughts then you'd never have any reason to get stressed at all. You'd simply block out all the unpleasant thoughts and live peacefully with all your happy thoughts.' I couldn't believe how obvious it sounded when he explained it like that. It was almost as if I already knew it at some level, but had somehow forgotten to apply the idea to my life. 'But what about productive thoughts?' I asked. 'What about creative thoughts, ones that are necessary to solve problems?'

'I'm not saying that all thinking is bad,' he said. 'We need the ability to think in order to live. It's the nature of mind to think. In the same way that the road was built for cars to journey on, so the mind exists to experience thoughts and feelings. So don't make the mistake of thinking that all thoughts are bad. They're not – we just need to know how to relate to them. What you need to ask yourself,' he continued, 'is how much of your thinking is helpful, productive, and how much is unhelpful or unproductive. Only *you* know the answer to that. I'm assuming that because you've come all this way to see me, your thinking causes you problems at times, that maybe some of it is not so helpful?' There was no arguing with that. A great many of my thoughts fell into the 'unhelpful and unproductive' category. 'If you're worried about losing these creative thoughts,' he gestured somewhat dismissively, 'then where do you think they come from in the first place? Do those moments of inspiration come from cold, rational thinking, or do they arise from the stillness and the spaciousness of the mind? When the mind is always busy there's no room for these thoughts to arise, so by training your mind you'll actually make *more* space for these creative thoughts to arise. The point is, don't be a slave to your mind. If you want to direct your mind and use it well, then good. But what use is the mind if it's all over the place, with no sense of direction or stability?'

Having thanked my teacher for his time I returned to my room to mull over all we'd discussed. Every point seemed to be as important as the next. For me it was a radically different way of approaching meditation, and I suspect it may well be for you too. But in that one short meeting I'd learnt that meditation, within a mindful context, was not about stopping thoughts and controlling the mind. It was a process of giving up control, of stepping back, learning how to focus the attention in a passive way, while simply resting the mind in its own natural awareness. My teacher had explained how it was a skill, an art, knowing how to step back and how not to get continually sucked into the realm of endless, unproductive and often stressful thinking. I'd learned how the thoughts were autonomous and how no amount of force could prevent them from arising.

Over the next few weeks I became increasingly enthusiastic about my meditation. This new way of approaching the same technique had been a revelation. It seemed to make a difference the very first time I tried it. Of course, sometimes I'd forget and slip back into my old habits, but slowly these new ideas started to take root. At times the mind continued to be very busy, just as my teacher had promised, but on other occasions it became very, very quiet. It was as if the volume of cars on the road had decreased to such an extent that I could now see the individual cars a lot more clearly. Not only that, but the space between these cars was now longer, wider, bigger. In fact, sometimes there appeared to be no cars at all. And it was then that I finally understood the confusion I'd experienced in learning meditation. Having heard about these moments of 'no thought' or 'empty space', I'd always assumed that it was something I had to *do*. As it turns out, though, it is in *not doing* that those moments arise. It is stepping back and allowing the mind to unwind in its own time and its own way that you will find a genuine sense of headspace.

The blue sky

So, how do you 'not do something', while engaged in an exercise that is designed to 'do something'? Despite the advice I'd received, this was an idea I still struggled with from time to time. Sure, sitting on the side of the road was fine for a little while, but before long I found myself impatiently waiting for more progress. It's hard to believe that a sense of calm was not enough to satisfy me, but I wanted more, I wanted insight. Because although the thoughts had started to settle down, I was still left with a lot of the usual emotional stuff. Whether it was feeling frustrated, worried or doubtful, these emotions seemed to cloud my experience of meditation time and time again. I also found it hard to believe that such a passive approach was really going to lead to any long-lasting change. It was one thing to experience a sense of calm in the monastery, but quite another to imagine this working among the chaos of everyday life. A good few months passed before I had the opportunity to see the senior teacher in the monastery again, but when I did I asked him if he could help me out with what was becoming an increasingly big obstacle for me.

'Imagine a clear blue sky,' he began. 'Feels nice, yes? It's very hard to feel down when the sky's blue like that.' He paused, as if to appreciate the space this image brought to the mind. 'Now, imagine that your mind is like this blue sky. I'm not talking about all the thoughts, confusion and craziness,' he said chuckling. 'I'm talking about the underlying essence of mind, the natural state.' I took a moment to think about it. Imagining a clear blue sky was one thing, but imagining that it somehow represented my own mind was quite another. There was nothing clear about my mind back then, it was just full of thoughts and confusing emotions. 'It doesn't matter whether this is your experience right now,' he said, 'simply "imagine" for a moment that this is how things are. In fact, think back to the last time you felt very happy and relaxed and it's probably not so very difficult to imagine.' He was right, when I thought about a happy time in my life at the same moment, it was actually very easy to imagine. Try it for yourself right now.

'OK,' he said, 'now imagine a very cloudy day, no blue sky at all, just big, dark, heavy clouds.' He said each word very slowly, as if to emphasise the point. 'How does that make you feel?' he asked, still smiling, 'not so good, right? Now, imagine those clouds are the thoughts in your mind, how sometimes they're fluffy and white and appear quite friendly, whereas at other times they appear dark and heavy. The colour of the clouds simply reflects your feeling or mood at the time.' It was true – when I had lots of friendly thoughts racing around, the fluffy white clouds, I wasn't that bothered about having a busy mind. Unless I was trying to meditate that is, and then I'd struggle with them sometimes. But when the thoughts were difficult, the heavy dark clouds, I started to feel really uncomfortable.

But it was the next bit of his story that really resonated and that I hope will stay with you too for a long time to come. 'In order to get to this monastery you must have flown in a plane?' he asked, knowing full well what the answer would be. I agreed. 'Was it cloudy when you left?' he asked. 'It's always cloudy in England,' I replied, smiling. 'Well then,' he said, 'you'll know that if you get in a plane and fly up through the clouds, there's nothing but blue sky on the other side. Even when it appears as though there's nothing but big, dark, heavy clouds, there's always blue sky there.' There was no denying it, I'd flown a lot over the years and he was right. 'So,' he said, shrugging his shoulders, 'the sky is always blue.' He chuckled to himself as though everything I ever needed to know was in that one sentence, and in a way it was.

I returned to my room and thought about the significance of what

I'd heard. As a concept I got it: the sky is always blue. The clouds are our thoughts and when the mind is very busy with all these thoughts the blue sky is temporarily obscured. In my own case, the mind had been so busy with thoughts, and for such a long time, that I'd almost forgotten what blue sky looked like. But it was more than that. It was this idea that the underlying essence of the mind, like the blue sky, is unchanging, no matter how we feel. When we're in a bad mood or feeling rough for some reason, then the cloud is simply more obvious, more distracting. There might be just the one thought in the entire sky, but it seems to demand every last bit of our attention.

The reason this lesson was so important for me – and I hope will be for you – was that I'd always assumed I had to somehow *create* blue sky. I was under the impression that to experience headspace I needed to make something happen. The truth is, we don't need to create anything. The blue sky is headspace, and it's always there – or, rather, *here*. This changed everything for me. Meditation was no longer about trying to create an artificial state of mind, which I'd imagined headspace was. Neither was it about trying to keep all the clouds at bay. It was more a case of setting up a deckchair in the garden and watching as the clouds rolled by. Sometimes the blue sky would peek through the clouds, which felt nice. And, if I was able to sit there patiently and not get too engrossed in the clouds, then even more of the blue sky would start to appear. It was as if it happened on its own, with no help from me whatsoever. Watching the clouds in this way gave me perspective, a sense of space that I'd not known in my meditation before. More than that though, it gave me the confidence to sit and rest my mind in its natural state, not trying, not doing, just being.

Of course, it's all very well me telling you this, but until you experience it for yourself it may not sound all that significant. But take a moment to imagine what it would be like to have that kind of freedom and space in your mind. Imagine what it would be like to be unconcerned with the volume or intensity of thoughts in your mind. Most of all, imagine what it would be like to have a place within your own mind which is always calm, always still and always clear; a place that you can always return to, a sense of being at ease or at peace with whatever is happening in your life.

Exercise 3: physical sensations

Put the book down for another couple of minutes and try this short exercise. We return here to the idea of being at peace with whatever is on your mind. Whereas last time you were focusing on sounds or visual objects, this time try focusing on a physical sensation. It can be the sensation of the body pressing down on the chair beneath you, the soles of the feet against the floor, or even the sensation of your hands resting on the book. The advantage of focusing on the physical sensation of touch like this is that it's very tangible, but you may well find that the mind still wanders a lot. If you do experience a very busy mind or a strong emotion of some kind, remember the idea of the blue sky, the possibility that perhaps underneath all those thoughts and feelings there might exist a place that is still, spacious and clear. So each time you realise the mind has wandered off and you've become distracted, just effortlessly move the attention back to the physical sensation.

The wild horse

Sometime later I found myself living in a much busier monastery, which served the needs of the local community and received a lot of visitors. We were still given many hours a day to meditate in a formal way, but the emphasis at this monastery was more on the practice of awareness in everyday life – in other words, the practice of mindfulness. Having previously had the luxury of moving seamlessly from one meditation session to the next, I'd grown accustomed to my mind settling quite quickly when I sat down to meditate. But now the sessions were often sandwiched between other activities, such as gardening, cooking, cleaning and paperwork. Often this involved working with others, having conversations and discussions about all sorts of things. Some of these conversations were monastic in nature and others were, how shall I say, less monastic. What I discovered very quickly was that this type of interaction made for a very different type of meditation session afterwards. Rather than sitting down and the mind immediately settling as it had before, it was now often very busy.

Falling back into my old habits of trying to control the mind (never underestimate the strength of this tendency), if my mind hadn't settled within five minutes or so, I started to resist the thoughts. And in resisting them I created yet more thoughts. I'd then panic about the fact that I was creating more thoughts and in doing so create even more thoughts!

I was fortunate enough to have a very experienced teacher on-hand again, and so went to ask his advice. He was known for his warm and often humorous teaching style and rarely answered a question with a straightforward answer. In fact, he would often answer a question with another question! But when he did answer, it was almost always in the form of a story, of which just like the previous teacher, he seemed to have an inexhaustible supply. I explained my difficulties as he sat listening, slowly nodding his head.

'Have you ever seen a wild stallion broken in?' he asked. I shook my head. What had that got to do with anything? He seemed a little disappointed, but then I guess life on the Tibetan steppes as a child is somewhat different from growing up in a small English village. He continued to talk about these wild horses, which he said were very difficult to catch and even harder to tame. 'Now, imagine you grab hold of one of these horses and try to keep it in one place,' he continued. I imagined standing next to the horse, holding on to it tightly with a rope. 'Impossible!' he blurted out, 'no man or woman can hold down a wild horse, it's too strong. Even if you got together with all your friends you'd never be able to hold it down in one place. This is not the way to tame a wild horse. When you first catch one of these horses,' he continued, 'you need to remember that they are used to running free. They're not used to standing still for a long time, or being forced against their will to stay in one place.' I started to get a sense of where he might be going. 'Your mind is like this wild horse when you sit to meditate,' he said, 'you can't expect it to stay still in one place all of a sudden just because you're sitting there like a statue doing something called meditation! So when you sit down with this wild horse, this wild mind, you need to give it lots of room. Rather than trying to immediately focus on the object of meditation, give your mind time to settle, to relax a little. What's the hurry?'

Again, he was right, I was rushing my meditation, thinking that somehow the next moment was more important than this one, still trying to get to a certain state of mind. Quite what point I was trying to reach was not entirely clear. 'Instead,' he suggested, 'approach your mind in the same way that these wild horses are broken in. Imagine you're standing in the middle of a really big space, a large open field. Now the horse is on the end of a slack rope that you're holding on to, but it has all the space it needs. It doesn't feel as though it's being trapped or pinned down in any way.' I imagined the horse running freely in the field, as I stood there keeping a watchful eye on it, holding on loosely to the end of the rope. 'Now place one hand over the other and very gently shorten the length of the rope by bringing it in a bit. Not by much, but just a little bit.' He held his thumb and forefinger up, just half a centimetre between them, as if to emphasise the point. 'If you do this gently enough with a wild horse, it won't even notice the difference – it will still feel as though it has all the space in the world. Keep doing this, slowly bringing the horse closer, all the while keeping an eye on it, but giving it enough space to feel at ease and not too nervous.'

This made a lot of sense and simply imagining the process made me feel more relaxed. 'So,' he said, 'this is what you need to do with your mind when you sit down and find it's very busy. Take it slowly, be gentle and give it all the space that it needs. Allow the horse to come to a natural place of rest, where it feels happy, confident and relaxed staying in one place. Sometimes it might struggle at first, but that's fine, just loosen the rope again slightly, and gently repeat the process. If you meditate in this way then your mind will be very happy,' he said.

Remembering this simple story will make a huge difference to your meditation. In fact, why not check out the horse-taming animation on our website at www.getsomeheadspace.com/headspace-book/get-some-headspace.

Meditation and Emotions

The reversal

With all this good advice, it wasn't long before my mind really started to settle down. There were still days when the mind was busy, but I was becoming increasingly comfortable with watching the thoughts as they passed by. The thoughts were somehow easier to deal with and I'd taken the analogies of the road and the blue sky to heart. However, when strong emotions arose in the mind or I started to feel physical discomfort, I had a hard time just sitting with it. I found it almost impossible to be unbiased in these situations. When I felt happy and blissed out I wanted to hold on to that feeling for as long as possible. But when unpleasant feelings arose I couldn't help but resist them. I'd lost count of how many times I'd been told that resistance was futile, that it only made the situation worse, but I just couldn't help myself.

This went on for some time. I saw it as a kind of heroic battle with the ego and, being quite stubborn, refused to back down. I didn't yet have the awareness to see that the only battle I was waging was against myself. Eventually I had to concede that I was getting nowhere and so once again I arranged to see my teacher. As I explained the situation to him, he nodded away as if he'd heard the same thing a hundred times before. 'It's the same for everyone,' he began. 'We're attracted to the things we like and we become attached to these things. We don't want to give them up for anything. The only problem is, the more we chase after them the further away they appear. And the more we try to hold on to these pleasant feelings, the more fearful we become of losing them.'

It was true. In fact, in my meditation practice it had even become a bit of an obstacle, because every time I had a session in which I experienced what I considered to be positive feelings it simply raised my expectations. This meant that when I came to the next session, far from sitting there *in the moment*, I was trying to recreate an experience from earlier on. 'At the same time as trying to hold on to the good things,' he continued, 'we're also busy trying to get rid of all the unpleasant things. It doesn't matter whether we're trying to get rid of lots of thoughts, difficult emotions, or a painful feeling in the body, it's all the same, it's resistance. And as long as there's resistance, there's no room for acceptance. And as long as we don't have acceptance, there's no way of having a peaceful mind.' It sounds so obvious when it's put like this, doesn't it? 'Happiness is just happiness,' he went on, 'no big deal. It comes and it goes. Sadness is just sadness, no big deal. It comes and it goes. If you can give up your desire to always experience pleasant things, at the same time as giving up your fear of experiencing unpleasant things, then you'll have a quiet mind.'

As I listened to his explanation, I couldn't help thinking that there was something missing. Sure, 'let go of attachment' and 'let go of resistance', but how? 'Simple. By becoming more aware,' he said. This seemed to be the answer for everything, and although I could see that my perspective was changing as my awareness grew, it didn't feel as though it was happening fast enough. I shared my thoughts with the teacher and he laughed, 'Ah,' he said, 'I think you're talking about *impatience*.' I shrugged my shoulders and nodded. 'I'd just like to know how to deal with these things until my awareness becomes a bit stronger,' I said. 'Perhaps there's another technique which could help?' I asked hopefully. He seemed to study me before answering. 'I want you to continue to focus on the breath, just practising how to rest in the natural awareness of your mind. However, there is *one* thing you could add to that exercise which might help in the meantime.' I raised my eyebrows in anticipation. He went on to explain, and you may well want to try this in your own meditation.

'When you experience pleasant sensations in your practice, I want you to imagine sharing those feelings with other people,' he began. 'It doesn't matter whether it's the pleasant sensation of a quiet mind, of a relaxed body or a comforting emotion; simply imagine you are giving it away, sharing it with your friends and family, the people you care about.' He continued. 'It doesn't require lots of thought and I still want you to focus on the breath, just counting the breaths as they pass. But, if you find yourself sitting there and you feel very good, then maintain this attitude of wanting to share it with others.' I couldn't really see how this was going to help, but it sounded harmless enough and the sentiment was well meaning. 'This next bit might be a little more challenging,' he said, smiling broadly. 'When you experience discomfort in your meditation, whether it's the restlessness of a busy mind, physical tension in the body, or a challenging emotion, I want you to imagine it's the discomfort of the people you care about. It's as if in an act of extraordinary generosity, you are sitting with their discomfort so they don't have to.'

It sounded bizarre. How could that help? Why would I want to give away the nice feelings and imagine sitting with the discomfort of others? 'Relax,' he said, 'it's not actually happening. But if you think about it, it's a very skilful way of working with the mind. When we try hard to hold on to pleasant states of mind that creates tension. By imagining you're giving away those feelings, and sharing them, you lose that tension and become less judgmental.' OK, that made sense, but what about the other part? 'When it comes to unpleasant feelings we're always trying to get rid of them, right? This also creates tension. This way we're doing the opposite of what we normally do, which means there's no resistance. And no resistance means no tension.' I thought about it, it made a certain amount of sense. In fact, it sounded like an elaborate version of reverse psychology. I guess the interesting thing was that it trained the mind to be more altruistic at the same time.

I went away and put the instructions into practice. I didn't need to change the exercise in any way, it was more about the approach to the technique and remembering to maintain the attitude of being less judgmental about the experience of meditation. Despite my doubts, my teacher had been right. When I had the attitude of sharing pleasant sensations they seemed to last longer, and the meditation became more enjoyable. It's hard to say what changed exactly, but I guess it became a little less self-serving. The other aspect was equally effective. I can't say that unpleasant emotions or tension immediately disappeared when I applied this method, but the intention had been to find a way to sit with those feelings with a greater sense of confidence and acceptance. And it was true, by imagining that I was doing something beneficial for others, it seemed to make the whole thing easier. This approach to the practice made a considerable difference to my ability and willingness to understand all aspects of the mind. Before that time I'd only wanted to get to know the pleasant sensations and had always feared unpleasant ones. But this changed everything; it was like seeing and understanding a part of my mind that I'd never seen before – and of course I'd never seen it because I was always so busy running away from it.

Exercise 4: focusing on pleasant or unpleasant sensations

Try it right now to see how it feels. Put the book down for a couple of minutes again and use a physical sensation to focus on as you gently close the eyes. Rather than using a neutral sensation as you did last time, focus on either a pleasant or unpleasant feeling in the body. For example, maybe you feel a lightness in your hands or feet, or perhaps you feel some tension in your shoulders. Normally you'd probably try to resist the feeling of discomfort and hold on to the feeling of comfort, but what happens when you reverse it and apply the principle of sharing pleasant feelings with others and sitting with difficult feelings on behalf of others? Does it change the experience? Remember, if you are focusing on a pleasant sensation try gently to maintain the attitude of sharing it with others as you focus on it. Equally, if you're resting your attention on an unpleasant feeling, then try to lightly maintain the attitude of experiencing it or looking after it for someone you care about.

What goes down, must come up

When I look back at my reasons for becoming a monk, I can't pick out the exact moment when I started to feel unhappy, but there was a series of events that undoubtedly 'tipped me over the edge'. By my late teens my mum had remarried and, along with a step-dad, my sister and I gained a step-sister and step-brother. Not long after, our step-sister, Joanne, was killed while out riding her bike, run over by a man in a van who was unable to stay awake at the wheel. The impact it had on the family is indescribable and yet I didn't really stop for long enough to take it in. Unable and unwilling to look at the amount of sadness around me, I just kept going. In fact, I even went away physically, as though that might somehow remove me from the feeling. Whilst the feeling didn't go away as such, it did at least allow me to live in ignorance for a little longer.

Then, a few months later I heard that an ex-girlfriend of mine had died while having heart surgery. I remember receiving the news and almost brushing it off as if it didn't matter. I thought that part of growing into a man was being able to deal with things in a detached kind of way. Unable to be with the feeling, I did the only thing I knew how and rammed it down inside.

They say these things come in threes, and sure enough soon afterwards number three arrived. I went to a party with a group of friends on Christmas Eve. After midnight we left in varying states of inebriation. It was a happy time, and everyone stood around hugging goodbye and wishing each other a merry Christmas. As I wandered off with a couple of friends I heard the sound of a car coming over the top of the hill. I remember looking and wondering why it didn't have its lights on. The car got faster and faster, speeding down the hill. Halfway down the man behind the wheel, who was later discovered to be more than four times over the limit, lost control of the car. Narrowly missing the three of us, the car veered on to the pavement and ploughed straight into the middle of the group of friends. It was a scene of utter devastation. The whole thing seemed to slow down to a frame-by-frame series of events, as if a camera were taking one shot after the next. In one shot there was the point of impact, the bodies of friends flung into the air like rag dolls. In another shot a body, lying slumped against the wall. Several people died that night and many more were seriously injured. Never in my life have I felt more helpless.

Whether it was through sheer grit and will-power, or the fear of what might happen if I lifted the lid of the pressure cooker, I managed to keep down the feelings that came after these events for quite some time. But after a year or so they started to come out in other ways, colouring the world around me. When it comes to emotions it's the case that whatever goes down, must come up. It might come to the surface as the emotion itself, or it might start to affect our behaviour in some way. Sometimes it can even affect our physical health. Stress-related health symptoms are increasingly common and widely acknowledged to be a result of our inability to deal with challenging feelings presented by a stressful situation or environment.

Locating emotion

By the time I got to the monastery these emotions were most definitely coming to the surface. Sometimes the feeling would be more obvious and the thoughts accompanying the feeling made it very clear what it was about, but more often it was just a feeling that arose. When I started to become aware of this sadness I felt a little hard done by. This wasn't what I'd signed up for. I'd signed up for peace and tranquillity in the mountains. For quite some time I continued to 'do battle' with these feelings, trying to ignore or resist them. The irony that I was doing this at the same time as trying to let go of ignorance and resistance escaped me altogether. Not being able to control the feeling I became frustrated, thinking it must be a lack of progress in my meditation. I started to think that maybe I wasn't cut out for meditation. I also became increasingly anxious whenever I sat down to meditate.

One day I decided I'd had enough and went to see the teacher. I explained what had been going on in my practice and he listened very patiently. Now I fully expected him to give me some secret technique developed especially to deal with difficult emotions, but instead he asked me a question.

'Do you like it when someone makes you laugh?' he asked. 'Of course,' I replied smiling. 'What about when someone makes you cry? Do you like that?' 'No,' I said, shaking my head. 'OK,' he continued, 'so let's say that I could show you how to never experience sadness again, would you like that?' 'Of course,' I nodded eagerly. 'The only condition is that you would also lose the ability to laugh as well,' he said, suddenly looking very serious. He seemed to read my thoughts. 'They are a package,' he said, 'you can't have one without the other. They are like two sides of the same coin.' I thought about it. 'Stop thinking about it,' he said, now laughing. 'It's impossible, I couldn't show you how to do it even if you wanted me to.'

'So what am I supposed to do?' I asked, 'if I can't get rid of this feeling of being sad all the time, how am I ever going to be happy?' His demeanour became more serious. 'You're looking for the wrong kind of happiness,' he said. 'True happiness doesn't distinguish between the kind of happiness you get from having fun and the sadness you feel when something goes wrong. Meditation is not about finding this kind of happiness. If you want to find this kind of happiness then go to a party. The kind of happiness that I'm talking about is the ability to feel comfortable no matter *what* emotion arises.' 'But how can I feel comfortable with feeling unhappy?' I shot back.

'Try looking at it this way,' he went on, 'these feelings are part of being human. Now maybe you know some people who seem a bit happier than you, and other people who are a bit more unhappy than you.' I nodded. 'So sometimes we're predisposed to feel a certain way,' he continued, 'some people a bit happier and some people a bit unhappier. But it's what's underneath that matters. Because neither person can control their feelings. The happy person cannot "keep hold" of his or her happiness and the unhappy person cannot "push away" his or her unhappiness.' While this wasn't the concise magic answer I'd gone to the teacher hoping for, it at least made sense.

He continued. 'Tell me what emotion is causing you most trouble right now?' 'Mostly it's feeling sad,' I replied, 'but that makes me feel worried about my meditation, and then I get angry because I can't stop feeling sad or worried.' 'OK, forget about the worry and the anger for a moment,' he said, 'we can deal with those later. Besides, these are just your reactions to the sadness. Let's look at the original emotion, sadness. How does it make you feel?' I thought the answer was fairly obvious. 'It makes me feel sad.' 'No,' he shot back, 'this is your *idea* of how it makes you feel, how you *think* it makes you feel, rather than how it *actually* feels.'

I dug my heels in a little further. 'No, it *actually* feels sad,' I said. 'OK,' he replied, 'so where is it?' 'Where's what?' I asked, now a little confused. 'Where's the sadness?' he replied. 'Is it in your mind or is it in your body?' 'It's everywhere,' I said. 'Are you sure?' he persisted. 'Have you looked to try and find this feeling, to try and find where it lives?' I'd been so caught up thinking about it that the idea of studying it had never occurred to me. I shook my head a little sheepishly. 'OK,' he said, 'so this is the first job. Go and find this feeling of sadness for me and then we can talk about it some more.' The meeting was clearly over.

Over the next few weeks I spent a lot of time trying to find this feeling of sadness. Although it seemed to colour the thoughts in my mind, I couldn't say that the sadness was the thoughts themselves. Besides, the thoughts were so intangible, I couldn't even really get a sense of them living anywhere permanently anyway. It did seem to be the case that when I thought about certain things it seemed to intensify the feeling of sadness, but that's not what he'd asked me to find. So I started to examine the body during my meditation (mentally that is), scanning up and down through the body and trying to find this thing called sadness. It was illusive, that's for sure. But there was definitely a certain quality about the physical sensations that gave me enough confidence to go back and say that the emotion of sadness lived in the body.

'So,' my teacher said chuckling, as he invited me into his office. 'Did you find what you were looking for?' 'Well, yes and no,' I replied. 'I couldn't find sadness in my mind, in the thoughts, although the sadness did seem to colour and influence my thinking.' He nodded. 'But I felt that there were certain places in the body where I could feel it more strongly, where it felt like something a little more tangible.' Again, he nodded. 'The problem,' I continued, 'was that every time I thought I'd found it, it seemed to shift to a different part of the body.' He smiled and nodded in agreement. 'Yes,' he said, 'it's hard to study something when it keeps changing like that. Where did you decide this sadness was?' he asked, raising his eyebrows. 'I guess I felt it mostly here,' I said, pointing to my chest. 'Anywhere else?' he asked. 'Well, maybe here a bit too,' I said, this time pointing to the area around my diaphragm. 'What about your ears?' he asked laughing, 'And what about your toes? Did you find any sadness there?' He was clearly having some fun, but he was right, I'd not found any sadness in my ears or my toes. In fact, I think I may have even neglected to look there. 'So,' he continued, 'you say this sadness lives around here,' he said, gesturing to my chest, 'but where *exactly*? You need to be more specific. And if it *does* live there, what size is it, what shape is it? Study it some more and then we can talk about it.'

Once again I went away and tried to pin down the sadness. One thing that I'd noticed during this time of watching the feeling was that the intensity of it seemed to have decreased. I wasn't sure if this was coincidental or not, but there was a definite change. Anyway, I went back to looking for sadness as instructed. It was tricky, because it didn't really seem to have any obvious shape or size. Sometimes it felt quite spacious, whereas at other times it felt more constricted. Sometimes it seemed to have quite a heavy quality about it and at other times it seemed to feel a bit lighter. Even when I thought I'd located a very clear and definite feeling, it was very hard to locate a central point. And as soon as I found a central point and focused on that, I realised that there must be a central point to that too. It felt endless. The one thing I couldn't ignore was that the intensity of emotion was continuing to diminish. There was now no question in my mind that by replacing the thoughts with simple awareness, something had happened, something had changed. I wondered if it was just a trick, if all along he'd known that I wasn't going to find anything. I intended to ask him next time we met.

I'm not sure if I looked different, but he seemed to recognise I was feeling less sad as soon as I opened the door. I explained what had happened as he listened patiently. When I suggested that it might have been a trick to get me to stop thinking about it all the time he laughed loudly and rocked back and forwards on his cushion. 'Very funny trick,' he said. 'No, it was no trick. When you came here I said that meditation would teach you to be more aware, I never said it would get rid of unpleasant emotions. It just so happens that when you're more aware there is very little room for these unpleasant emotions to operate. When you're thinking about them all the time, then of course you give them lots of room, you keep them active. But if you don't think about them, then they tend to lose their momentum.'

'So, it *was* a trick,' I replied. 'No trick!' he exclaimed, 'did you find the sadness you were looking for?' 'Well, no, not really,' I replied. 'Exactly,' he said, with a smile on his face, 'I'm not saying that these feelings do or do not exist, but you've found for yourself that when you study the emotion very closely, it's actually very hard to find. This is something to remember when you find yourself reacting strongly to an emotion. When you came you said that not only did you feel sad, but you also felt frustrated and worried about your meditation. But these emotions were nothing but your reaction to the original emotion, making the whole situation that much worse. What about now, did you experience anger or worry when you were simply watching the sadness with awareness?' I shook my head in reply. He was right, I'd not experienced any. I'd felt frustrated at times at not being able to find what I was supposedly looking for, but certainly not worried. In fact, I'd started to look forward to the meditation again and even found myself laughing a few times at the fact that I couldn't seem to find this thing that was supposedly causing me so much trouble. 'Exactly,' he said again, this time with an even bigger smile on his face, 'why would you react very strongly when you can't even find a feeling there to react to? In order to resist something you need to have an idea of what it is. Often our "idea" of a feeling is just that, an idea. When we look a little more closely, we see that the idea is actually not what we thought it was. This makes it very difficult to resist. And with no resistance, there is simply acceptance of the emotion.'

I won't pretend that this process was quick, or easy, and nor did it mark the end of me feeling unpleasant emotions. But the experience taught me some lessons. One of the most important was that the emotion itself is often not the problem. It's the way we react to it that causes the problem. For example, I feel angry and respond to it with more anger, stoking the coals, keeping the fire of anger burning.

Or I feel worried and I start to feel worried that I feel worried. By stepping back and getting a little bit of perspective (something I could never have done without meditation) I was able to see the original emotion for what it was. And by simply being aware of it, it was as if it had its moment in the sun and was more willing to move on. So often we shut down when unpleasant feelings arise, we don't want to feel them or be around them. But by reacting in this way we only give the emotion a greater sense of importance.

By learning to let emotions come and go, and because there's this underlying sense of awareness and perspective, then no matter how difficult the feeling, there is always the sense that everything is OK, even if the emotion is very strong. The other lesson I learned was that sometimes, the 'idea' of something can be very different from reality. I thought I felt very sad, but when I tried to locate that sadness, all I could find were these ever-changing thoughts and physical sensations. I struggled to find any permanent emotion. I just found thoughts and physical sensations that were coloured by the feeling.

Fleeting emotions

Often we're simply unaware of our feelings. Sure, we notice them when they're raging out of control, at either end of the spectrum, but the rest of the time it's as though they're just there in the background colouring our view of life. But also the speed at which our emotions change, one feeling morphing into the next, can make them seem impossible to separate and define. Think back to the last time you felt happy, do you remember when it began? Take a minute or so to see if you can pinpoint the very moment the emotion of happiness came into being. And then when did it end? What about the last time you felt angry? You might remember the situation or context for the anger, but can you remember when the feeling of anger began and when it finished? And what caused these emotions to suddenly vanish? Was it that they ran out of steam? Did something else more important grab your attention? Or was it simply replaced by the next feeling?

For something that's so central to our entire experience of life, we have remarkably little understanding of emotions. Neuroscientists can tell us with amazing accuracy what's happening physiologically, and behavioural scientists can interpret that data to give us a rational explanation for why we feel the way we do. But although this is helpful and interesting, does it change the way you feel? More importantly, does it alter the way you respond or react to the way you feel? I may know that I shouldn't get angry because it releases harmful chemicals into my body and causes my blood pressure to rise, but that knowledge does little to stop me getting angry. Likewise, I know that taking it easy and being a bit more carefree will make me feel less stressed, but that is of little use if I'm going out of my mind with worry. Sometimes this gap between what we understand intellectually, and our actual experience of emotions in everyday life, can appear as an enormous chasm.

Just as my teacher asked me to consider a life without emotions, good or bad, can you truly say you'd want to live without emotion? The way we feel is fundamental to our experience of life. Perhaps in those moments when we're overcome by a difficult emotion we might wish that there was some way to get rid of all of them, but this is usually fleeting.

People often begin learning meditation either trying hard to get *rid* of emotions, or fearful that meditation might turn them into some kind of disinterested grey blob, with no sense of emotion whatsoever. But as we've seen, this isn't the case at all.

The filter of emotions
Emotions affect our perception of people, of situations and the environment in which we live. As a direct consequence, they also affect

our *relationships* with people, situations and the environment in which we live. Emotions are the filter between 'us' and the 'world'.

When we feel angry the world can look very threatening: we see situations as obstacles and other people as enemies. And yet when we feel happy, the world can appear as quite a friendly place. We view the same situations as opportunities and the same people as friends. The world around us has not changed that much, but our experience of that world is radically different.

When I think of this idea of a filter I'm reminded of my favourite place to go on holiday. It's a rugged place, next to the sea, where the forces of nature are strong and the weather changes often. From the chair where I like to sit, I can see an enormous ridge of rock that towers above the village and the beach and stretches out into the ocean. On a clear sunny day these cliffs look spectacular. They appear deep red in colour and have a sense of majesty about them. Even from a distance it's possible to make out every small detail. On a day like this the rock is truly awe-inspiring. But when it's a little more cloudy, the appearance of the rock changes frequently throughout the day. Sometimes it looks dull, almost a matt brown in colour, as the shadow of the clouds linger. At other times it seems to take on a yellow, sulphurous tinge. If the clouds are quite dark it can even appear green. Sometimes, on a really stormy day, the cliffs take on a whole different quality altogether. They look almost black in colour and the sharp angles along the top of the ridge seem to carve their way in the sky. On days like this the rock appears imposing, even menacing, in nature. Just as before, the 'rock' has not changed in any way, it's simply that the clouds that pass overhead create the illusion that the rock is somehow different. In the same way, the filter of emotion creates the illusion of how our world looks at any one time.

But there's another aspect of emotion which differentiates a fleeting experience of happiness or sadness, for example, from a more ingrained, habitual feeling of happiness or sadness. In the context of meditation this is sometimes discussed in terms of 'traits' and 'states'.

Traits

Traits are those emotions that seem to define a character. It might be 'cheerful Amy' or 'moody Mark'. These traits can reflect our upbringing, social conditioning, and the experiences that have shaped us along the way. It's as if they are part of our genetic code and they tend to feel very 'set' in nature. Because of this, many people are not even that aware of their own traits.

Take a moment to think what your traits might be. You might consider what your view of life is like. Does it feel as though life is working *with* you or *against* you? Does life feel like a *pleasure* or a *chore*? For meditation to be effective, it doesn't matter which it is – although you may well find the former a considerably more enjoyable way to live. And what about your friends, family and work colleagues? I'm sure you can think of people at either end of the 'perspective scale'. At one end you'll have the person who's capable of putting a negative spin on just about anything – winning the Lottery, finding love, getting a promotion. They might get very angry sometimes, or simply moan and grumble their way through life. At the other end of the spectrum, there are those who appear so overwhelmingly cheery that you find yourself asking 'Is this person for real?' Of course, sometimes they're not 'for real', but there are undoubtedly some people who seem naturally happy and content in life. So these emotions can be compared to character traits.

States

'States' however refer to those fleeting emotions that come and go in everyday life. Perhaps someone says something unpleasant to you, your child takes their first steps, or you get some bad news. These things are likely to be met with the appropriate emotion that will come and then go again, they are the 'ups and downs' of life. You might experience a burst of anger at a driver on the road, but before you've had a chance to indulge the story, something on the radio has grabbed your attention and you find yourself laughing, the anger forgotten. Or it might be something more serious, perhaps a long period of depression after losing your job, which seems to hang around for some time before leaving. Either way, the fact that the feeling comes and goes in this way indicates that they are temporary 'states', as opposed to 'traits'. Sometimes our emotional states can become so ingrained, they start to feel like traits. It's as if the emotion is so over-whelming that we can't see past it. And in these situations the emotion can even begin to define who we are. Depression is a good example of this. So while at times the two can feel insepa-rable, it's useful to be aware of the difference.

Headspace and emotions

Having experimented with a number of different meditation tech-niques over the years, I still feel that the clearest, simplest and most widely accessible approach to emotions is the same approach that we discussed in relation to thought. After all, it's very difficult to separate thought and feeling. Do your thoughts define the way you feel? Or does the way you feel define your thoughts? Mindfulness is the willingness to rest in that natural state of awareness, resisting the temptation to judge whatever emotion comes up, and therefore neither opposing or getting carried away with a feeling. Meditation is simply the exercise that is going to give you the best conditions to practise being mindful of these emotions. And headspace is the result of applying this approach. Headspace does not mean being *free* from emotions, but rather existing in a place where you are at ease with whatever emotion is present.

In the same way that we defined thoughts as neither 'good' nor 'bad', we're going to do the same with feelings. Now this idea is usually met with 'What the . . . ? How can you tell me that anger's not bad? I just shouted at someone, surely that has to be bad? And it feels horrible. When I'm angry I feel like I want to explode! What's "good" about anger?' Well, of course the consequences of anger are a very different matter and it's important to exercise restraint, but in the context of this exercise it helps to adopt an open mind, one that is curious and interested in the nature of the emotion itself, rather than simply labelling the emotion as good or bad through past experience. Otherwise we're left with the same old attitude of chasing after 'positive' emotions and trying to get rid of all the 'negative' ones. Only you can say how well that approach has worked for you so far.

So we come back to the idea of gentle curiosity: watching, observing and noticing what happens in the body and mind as these emotions come and go. Remember, the objective here is headspace, a sense of ease with whatever emotion is present. It means to sit on the roadside, watching the emotions pass, neither getting drawn into them because they look inviting, nor running away from them because they look frightening. The technique is not about trying to stop *emotions* from arising, in the same way that it's not about trying to stop *thoughts* from arising. Like thoughts, emotions spontaneously arise. It's how we meet these emotions, how we respond to them that is important.

When approaching emotions through meditation, it's not that we need to give the emotions more importance (they already receive quite enough attention); instead, we need to find a way to relate to them in a more skilful way. We need to find a way to be aware of our emotions, to experience, acknowledge and live with them, and yet not be at their mercy. Mindfulness and meditation show us how best to do this.

At an intellectual level, we can also appreciate the value of so-called negative emotions. I often hear people say that were it not for a particularly difficult period in their life, they would never have gone on and done the things they've done – and that even if they could go back and change it, they wouldn't. With the passing of time and with increased perspective, the experience of emotion can look very different.

It's the nature of life for stuff to happen. And when it happens it can be good to know that you're as well equipped as you can be to deal with the situation. This doesn't mean that you won't experience the feeling, because undoubtedly you will. But what it *does* mean is that the way in which you relate to the feeling will enable you to let go of it more quickly and more easily.

Exercise 5: being aware of your feelings

We're not always very good at recognising how we are feeling. That's usually because we're distracted by what we're doing or what we're thinking. But when you start to meditate you inevitably start to become more aware of how you feel – the variety of feelings, the intensity of feelings, the stubborn nature of some emotions, and the fleeting nature of others. How do you feel right now, for example? Put the book down for a couple of minutes and close your eyes. It can be useful to notice how your body feels first, as that can give you a clue as to what the underlying emotion is. Does it feel heavy or does it feel light? Is there a sense of stillness or of restlessness in the body? And is there a sense of restriction or spaciousness? Rather than rush to decide, apply the idea of gentle curiosity and take a good 20 to 30 seconds to answer each question. And how does the breath feel in the body – does it feel fast or slow, deep or shallow? Without trying to change it, take just a few moments to notice how it feels. By the end of the exercise you'll most probably have a much better sense of how you feel emotionally. But don't worry if not, as that's perfectly normal at first and it will become more obvious with practice.

Gentle curiosity

When I first heard that meditation was simply a snapshot of my everyday mind I found it hard to believe. I'd never experienced my mind with quite so much awareness and so I'd never seen it that way before. On the one hand, there was a familiarity to it all, but on the other it was not what I was expecting at all. You may have already got a sense of this with your own mind, even from just those few short exercises I've outlined. When we meet something new or unexpected, we tend to react to it in a different way to those things that are familiar. Some react with excitement and wonder, others approach it with a sense of anxiety or trepidation. The same is true when it comes to watching the mind.

My own modus operandi when I started was one of bullishness. I was not really that interested in what happened along the way, I just wanted to experience the ultimate fruit of meditation – that of enlightenment. I guess you could call it an 'enlightenment or bust' kind of attitude, where I was always focusing on a future goal rather than resting in the moment and enjoying all that life had to offer. It's a common mistake to make in meditation, to search for some kind of experience or want to be rewarded with some sign of progress or fruition, but peace of mind or insight will always be illusive if we are trying too hard to find it.

When it comes to meditation, though, the goal and the journey are the same thing. So my approach to meditation was probably the equivalent of leaving home on a driving holiday, not stopping at any of the places on the way, driving through the night without a break and refusing to look out of the windows during the hours of daylight. It kind of defeats the purpose!

The qualities you bring to your own approach will always reflect your upbringing and your character. Some of these qualities you might like and find helpful, others may feel uncomfortable and decidedly unhelpful. But if you can bring a sense of genuine intrigue and curiosity to your meditation, then it doesn't really matter what those qualities are. That's because they become part of the meditation, part of that which is observed. One of my teachers always used to describe this quality as *gentle curiosity*. When this becomes part of your approach to meditation you'll notice that the mind feels very open. For example, you may well think, much like myself at the time, that if you've seen one breath then you've seen them all. And if this is your attitude to following the breath, then you'll undoubtedly lose interest very quickly. But if you take the time to look a little more closely, you'll notice that each and every breath is actually quite unique. The same can be said of the thoughts that pass through the mind (even if sometimes it feels as though it's the same one coming back time and again), and even physical sensations that arise in the body.

The idea of approaching meditation with a gentle curiosity seemed to me to imply a sense of soft, open and patient interest. It's perhaps the way in which you might quietly crouch behind a tree while watching a wild animal. Because you're so captivated and engaged, you're 100 per cent focused on what you're watching. You are aware of the immediacy of the moment, free from impatience, not wanting the animal to *do* something, but content to watch it just as it is. Or perhaps it's like watching an insect on the floor. At first you may look at it and think 'Oh, it's a bug.' But then you look a little closer and see all the legs. So you look a little closer again and see the features on the face. Each time you notice something new about this 'bug'. If you can apply this sense of gentle curiosity, to your meditation and even everyday life, it will add something that is every bit as beneficial as it is unexpected.

The hot soup

By way of contrast, I'd like to leave you with one final story before we move on to the topic of the practice itself. It involves my lack of gentle curiosity, a very strict monastery and some very hot soup.

Like many monasteries in the West, this place frequently opened its doors to visitors so that they could take part in short meditation retreats. During these periods we were expected to look after them as guests of the monastery. As part of their daily schedule they had breakfast and lunch delivered to their room. Although room service in a monastery may sound a little luxurious, it was to give the retreat participants the opportunity to practise 'eating meditation' (details of which you can find on page 130). So, as monks and nuns we'd take it in turns to prepare the food, put it on plates, and deliver it to the rooms. Lunch was simply a small bowl of soup and a piece of bread. The soups were all freshly made, often with ingredients from the garden, and were rotated throughout the week. We'd done quite a lot of retreats and I was getting used to just going through the motions as I prepared the soup and, if I'm honest, not really giving it my full attention. In fact, I became a little slapdash about it all – a bit of this, a bit of that, chuck it in, see what happens. I liked to think of it as creative flair, but in reality I was just too lazy to weigh everything out and create more washing-up. Besides, I figured the quicker I finished, the more time I'd have to rest.

One day I went into the kitchen and saw that mulligatawny soup was on the menu. It's a curry-based soup and one I'd made lots of times before. I set about cooking the vegetables, blending them together and making the broth. I'd made it so many times that I didn't bother using the recipe card any longer. I reached the point where I had to add in the herbs and the curry powder. Like many big kitchens, all the herbs and spices were stored in identical clear jars. In fact, the appearance of the contents and a simple sticky label on the front of the jar was the only way of telling them apart. Opening the cupboard, I reached in and took out the one with 'curry powder' labelled on the front. Noticing the reddish colour of the powder, I paused momentarily and thought how strange it looked, but then quickly pushed the thought aside. I was in far too much of a hurry to apply any gentle curiosity, I just wanted to get it finished so I could enjoy a bit more of the lunch-break. The idea that I could make the soup and enjoy myself at the same time hadn't even occurred to me.

Now when I was first taught to make the soup, I'd been instructed to taste it as I went along, to make sure it was OK. Not really paying close attention to the measurements and not bothering to taste it, I quickly spooned in the different ingredients. Thinking I'd spice it up a little to give it some more flavour, I chucked in a couple of heaped tablespoons. I continued to stir the ingredients, until it looked as though it was just about the right consistency and ready to serve.

I leaned over and smelt the soup. My nose bristled at the spice and my eyes immediately began to water. 'That's odd,' I thought, 'I don't remember it being like that before.' I picked up the spoon and took a mouthful. It felt as if my head was about to explode. I mean, I like things hot, I'd spent a lot of time living in Asia eating spicy food, but this was another level. In fact, I'd never tasted anything so hot in my life. Coughing and spluttering, I tried to cool my mouth by putting anything in it that I thought might help. I looked at the clock and saw that I only had five minutes before the soup had to be served up and on its way. Unfortunately, my new-found sense of calm in my meditation practice had yet to find its way into the more stressful situations of everyday life. So rather than take it in my stride, I started to panic.

I hurriedly thought back to the curry houses I used to go to after a night on the town as a student. All I could remember was the idea of balancing out heat with something cool and sweet. I grabbed the milk and poured it in. Nothing. So I tried a bit more. Nothing. And now it was going really runny. I started talking to myself as I was doing it. 'Yoghurt? Why not, chuck it in.' Still nothing. 'Apricot jam? Chuck it in.' Now that one did seem to work a little, although it gave the soup a very strange flavour. Working on the premise that sweet preserves of any kind were most definitely the way forward, in went the marmalade, honey and even the molasses. It was still burning hot, but at least it was now vaguely edible, albeit with a rather curious taste.

I quickly filled up the bowls and placed them outside each of the rooms, knocking just lightly to let them know that their lunch was ready. By now I'd started to calm down, but I knew what it was like to be in retreat, looking forward to your last meal of the day, only to be served something horrible. On the bright side, I realised it was only the second day of a week-long silent retreat, so I figured nobody could complain for another five days. 'Who knows . . .' I thought, 'maybe they'll have forgotten by the end of the week.' But seriously, who was going to forget that? Having an upset stomach is no fun at the best of times, but having it in a silent retreat when you're sharing one toilet between six other people is no fun at all.

It later transpired that in filling the jars of spices, somebody had accidentally mixed up the curry and chilli powder. So, rather than putting one level tablespoon of mild curry powder in the soup, I'd put two heaped tablespoons of chilli powder. Of course, in the big scheme of things no real harm had been done, but for me it epitomises the way we can sometimes plough through life, trying to get to the end of everything and not really paying attention to the journey. By taking the time to pause, and be curious, I could have so easily avoided the entire situation. Instead, I was so caught up in the pursuit of free time that I ploughed on through. Ironically, any free time I did have was then spent worrying about what I'd done. Sound familiar?

So, as you apply the instructions to your own meditation try, whenever you can, to apply this idea of gentle curiosity to whatever you're watching in the mind. It will make more of a difference than you could possibly imagine.

Exercise 6: mental body scan

A great way of cultivating this quality of gentle curiosity is to apply it to physical sensations within the body. Put the book down again and gently close your eyes as before. Starting at the top of the head, mentally scan through your body all the way down to the tips of your toes. The first time, do it quite quickly, taking about 10 seconds to go from head to toe. The next time, take a bit longer, more like 20 seconds. And then do it one final time in a bit more detail, taking about 30 or 40 seconds to do it. As you scan down through the body, notice which parts of it feel relaxed, comfortable and at ease, and which parts feel painful, uncomfortable or restricted in some way. Try to do it without any judgment or analysis, but more with a sense of just building up a picture of how the body feels right now. Don't worry if thoughts distract you every now and then – each time you realise the mind has wandered off you can gently bring it back to wherever you left off.

What the research shows

1 Medical professionals give their backing to mindfulness

In a recent study by the UK Mental Health Foundation, 68% of GPs agreed that it would be helpful for their patients to learn mindfulness-based meditation techniques – even for those without any health problems. The only difficulty is that most of these doctors said they didn't know where to find the appropriate mindfulness resources – enter Headspace.

2 Meditation activates parts of the brain related to happiness

If you're the kind of person who is very resilient and optimistic, then there's a good chance that the front *left*-hand side of your brain is very active. If, on the other hand, you tend to get quite anxious and caught up in lots of negative thinking, then it will be the front *right*-hand side of the brain which is more active. Neuroscientists at the University of Wisconsin found that after just eight weeks of mindfulness practice, participants experienced a significant change in the activity from right to left, which corresponded with increased feelings of happiness and wellbeing.

3 Mindfulness reduces the intensity of negative emotions

Neuroscientists from UCLA recently discovered that people who practise mindfulness techniques experience negative emotions less intensely than those who do not. They found that by 'labeling' these emotions and thereby becoming more aware of them, the intensity was significantly reduced. So, the next time you find yourself writing a retaliatory e-mail or wanting to shout at your partner in a fit of rage, label your anger 'anger' and you might just avoid having to make an embarrassing apology.

4 Meditation unwinds the harmful effects of stress

It's a well known fact that stress has a significant impact on our health. In the past, doctors have found that the 'stress response' can increase blood pressure, cholesterol levels, and even lead to strokes, hypertension and coronary heart disease. It also impacts the immune system and has been shown to reduce the chances of conception. In contrast, meditation has been shown to evoke the 'relaxation response', where blood pressure, heart rate, breathing rate and oxygen consumption all decrease, whilst the immune system is given a significant boost.

5 Mindfulness has been proven to reduce anxiety

A few years back the University of Massachusetts Medical School investigated the effects of mindfulness-based meditation on a group of people suffering with generalised anxiety disorder. An incredible 90% of the participants documented significant reductions in anxiety and depression, following just eight weeks of learning. Even more surprisingly, in a recent follow-up, three years after the initial experiment, the researchers found that these improvements had been maintained.

The Practice

There are thousands of different meditation techniques in the world, each coming from its own tradition and each with its own particular emphasis. However, at the heart of most of them is the intention to remain focused, relaxed, and with that natural quality of awareness I mentioned earlier. Another way of putting it might be 'the intention to rest in the moment'. Before you say, 'That doesn't sound like my mind at all, I'll never do it, my mind's all over the place', it's worth remembering that this is a skill you're learning. If you'd never played the piano before and went along for your first piano lesson, I doubt you'd take one look at the piano and then make a run for the door. I assume that's the whole reason you went for the lesson in the first place – to learn to play the piano. This is the same principle. It may well be that you feel as though your mind is all over the place, but that's why you're learning to meditate. It may sound obvious, but for some reason it's easy to forget this fact.

All meditation, no matter which culture or tradition it comes from, how complicated it might appear, or what its purpose might be, relies on at least one of two essential components: concentration (usually the calming aspect) and clarity (usually the insight aspect). Sometimes the technique might incorporate just one of these components and at other times it will incorporate both. What tends to differentiate meditation techniques is more often the approach and the desired outcome. For example, the technique might be designed to increase concentration, to generate devotion, develop compassion, improve performance, or any one of a whole number of possibilities. But all of these techniques still rely on at least one, if not both, of these two key components. Mindfulness is a great example of how these two different aspects can be brought together to create a broad and flexible technique very well suited to the demands of modern-day living. And so it is with Take10, the technique I'm about to teach you. It brings together both these components, but with a slightly greater emphasis on the calming aspect.

Have you ever noticed how quiet the mind becomes when you really focus on something? How, even if your mind is all over the place beforehand, once you're engaged in something you enjoy doing and are focused on that activity wholeheartedly, the mind starts to settle and feel calm? Well, meditation is a very similar process. To begin with we need to give the mind something to focus on, something to concentrate on. Traditionally these were known as 'objects of meditation' or 'meditation supports' and they were classified as external or internal. External supports might include techniques such as gazing at a particular object, listening to a particular sound, or perhaps chanting a particular word or phrase over and over again. This last one, known as a mantra, can also become an internal object, by simply repeating it in the mind rather than out loud. (Fear not, though, we won't be doing any chanting – that's really not the Headspace way.) Other internal objects of meditation might include focusing on the breath, bodily sensations, or even visualising a particular image in the mind.

For the purpose of Take10, I'm going to suggest that you use the breath as your primary support. There are many reasons for this, some of which I'll go into in more detail later, but first and foremost the breath is undoubtedly one of the most flexible meditation objects. Unlike chanting or staring at a candle, you'll be able to do this anywhere, even in public, without anyone else knowing what you're doing. The breath is with you wherever you go. And if it's not, then meditation is the least of your worries! But there's also something comforting in focusing on a physical sensation, as it helps to draw the attention away from the realm of thought and into something a bit more tangible.

Now for some people this is enough. Simply to sit each day, observe the breath, let the mind settle, and allow all the tension to work its way out of the system. And as I said earlier, there's nothing wrong in using meditation in this way, it's just that you won't be getting the full benefit. In order to get the very most from meditation, you'll probably want to integrate it with your everyday life. And in order to do that, you'll need to add the second component – clarity. This way you get to see what's causing the tension in the first place, you get to understand how and why you feel the way you do in certain situations. It's the difference between 'responding skilfully' to situations and 'reacting impulsively'. So, rather than getting to a point of stress and then needing to unwind, you can stop it happening in the first place – at least most of the time. I say you have to *add* clarity, but in fact that's not strictly true, because clarity naturally arises from a quiet mind.

The still pool of water

There was one particular monastery where I lived that was dedicated entirely to meditation. There was no study of any philosophy or psychology, it was all about the practice itself. There were no visitors, no phone calls, and very few distractions of any kind. We started meditation at 3 a.m. and then continued throughout the day (with a few breaks) until 10 p.m. in the evening. For someone wanting to devote all their time to meditation it was a dream come true. While this may sound a little extreme, it actually makes a lot of sense. The very reason I went off and became a monk was to train my mind in the most conducive environment possible, so limiting any distractions was simply the starting point for that process. And it's surprising, when the body and mind are starved of all the usual distractions, how even the smallest things can wreak havoc in the quiet of the mind. A simple letter from a friend can stir up all kinds of thoughts and emotions that can keep the mind entertained for days at a time. So, with none of these things to distract me, it's perhaps no surprise that my mind started to slow down and feel a little more settled. And when it did, what became immediately obvious was that the quieter the mind, the greater the clarity.

Over the years I've heard many ways of describing this process, but I think the analogy I'm going to share with you now works best. Imagine a very still, clear pool of water. The water is quite deep, but very, very clear. Because the water's so clear you can see absolutely everything at the bottom, making it appear shallow, even though it's actually very deep. Now imagine sitting by the side of this water and throwing small pebbles into the middle. Start off quite slowly, just throwing them every now and then. You'll notice that each new pebble creates a ripple on the surface of the water, and that it takes a little while for the water to then settle again. If you then throw another stone in before the water has completely settled, you create a new set of ripples that merges with the last. Now imagine throwing one stone after the next and seeing the entire surface of the water all stirred up at the same time. When the surface of the water looks like this, it's almost impossible to see anything in the water at all, never mind anything at the bottom.

This image reflects the surface of our minds in many ways – at least until we get round to training in some way. Each new thought, like a pebble being thrown into the water, creates ripples on the surface. We've got so used to throwing these pebbles, so used to the disturbance on the surface of the water, that we've forgotten what still water looks like. We know it's not quite right as it is, but it's as if the more we meddle with the mind trying to sort it out, the more ripples we create. It's this restless quality of mind that creates the feeling of agitation when we sit down and find ourselves unable to relax. Needless to say, when the mind's all stirred up like this, it's almost impossible to see what's happening and what's hidden under the surface. Because of this we don't have any insight into the nature of mind – of how and why we feel the way we do. So, without first calming the mind, it's very difficult to have any clarity. That's why there's slightly more emphasis on the concentration component in this particular technique.

I don't know about you, but I'd always assumed that clarity in meditation was all about lightning bolts of wisdom that would immediately transform my everyday experience. In retrospect, it is a slightly more gradual process. So maybe it's more useful to think about clarity in terms of a steady unfolding of the mind, an increasingly direct insight into what's happening. And this increasing clarity is vital. It's so hard to live life with a sense of ease and purpose if we're always in a muddle, confused and unable to direct the mind in a particular way. No matter how laid back we might be, we all have certain habitual tendencies that would benefit from a greater sense of awareness. Sometimes these seem to be hidden just under the surface, waiting to make a spectacular appearance when we're least expecting it. In fact, it can take just the smallest thing to happen, the most innocuous comment to be made, and that feeling rushes to the surface and colours the entire pool. Sound familiar? If we're ever going to study these feelings and emotions that both complicate and enrich our lives, then we need the surface of the water to be still enough so that we can see them.

The thing to remember about clarity is that what needs to become clear, will *naturally* become clear. Meditation is not about rooting around in the recesses of the mind, digging up old memories, getting caught up in analysis and trying to make sense of it all. That's not meditation, that's thinking – and we all know where thinking has got us up to now! Clarity arises in its own time and its own way. Sometimes clarity will mean becoming more aware of the thinking process. At other times the awareness might shift to the emotions or physical sensations. Whatever happens and whatever you become more aware of, allow it to happen naturally. So, instead of resisting it because it's unpleasant or uncomfortable, or trying to hasten its departure by delving into analysis, just allow it to happen in its own way and at its own pace.

Remember, these experiences are essentially the body and mind unwinding, releasing old baggage they've been carrying around for a long time. The fact you're seeing things more clearly, even if the experience is not always comfortable, is very, very good news – because this process is the process of letting go, and in letting go we get to feel a little lighter in life.

Check out our website www.getsomeheadspace.com/headspace-book/get-some-headspace for a short animation which very nicely illustrates this idea.

The lawn

Back in 'Colditz', the monastery from which I escaped over the wall, I was once asked to cut the grass. Now the grounds were quite big and there was a lot of land to cover, so naturally I went to the shed to get the lawnmower. But just as I was getting it out, one of the more senior monks came and presented me with a pair of scissors. 'What am I supposed to do with these?' I asked. 'You're supposed to cut the grass,' he replied, with slightly more relish than necessary. 'You've got to be having a laugh?' I said, 'That's going to take me for ever! What's the point in having a lawnmower if we don't use it?' He stared at me. 'First of all, you don't ever speak to me like that. And second of all, no, I'm not "having a laugh". The abbot has asked for you to cut the grass with these scissors and that's exactly what you're going to do.' I don't mind admitting that it took every ounce of self-restraint I had not to lose it with this guy. But he'd already got me into a lot of trouble with the abbot, so I wasn't going to push it, at least not this time. I walked away with the scissors in my hand thinking thoughts which, as a novice monk, I would most definitely not have been encouraged to think.

Cutting a lawn with a pair of scissors was a little bit like cutting hair. I took the grass between the middle finger and forefinger on my left hand, while I trimmed it with the scissors in my right. Everything had to be exactly level too, a feat that could only be achieved by pressing my cheek down into the lawn next to the part I was trimming. There were three lawns in total and this one alone was similar in size to a tennis court. Not surprisingly, after just a few minutes on the job I found myself trying to work out how long it was going to take me. I also started to think about my knees which were getting wet on the grass, my back which was hurting from bending over, and of course the monk who'd given me the scissors. In fact my mind was racing with thoughts. I had no sense of calm whatsoever and found it difficult to focus on the task at hand. And because I was still feeling so incensed, I had no clarity either.

In that moment, it was as if everything was coloured by anger. I don't know if you've ever experienced this, but it's as if all the thoughts that flash through the mind have this same angry quality that changes your entire perspective of the world around you. But I was so caught up in the thoughts, all the ripples on the surface of the water, that I couldn't see that at all. It was as if I were too close to the anger, identifying so strongly with it that I had *become* the anger, as opposed to just witnessing its presence. And without the clarity that the anger was actually coming from my own mind, I just looked for things to fuel that feeling. Sure, the attitude of the monk had not been great, but I was there of my own volition and I could have walked away if I'd wanted to. In many ways it was no different from being asked to do something unpleasant or boring in a shop, office, factory or any other place of work. In fact, you may have identified your very own 'grass cutting' moments already. While it's important to acknowledge that it is absolutely not OK to be walked over, abused, bullied or taken for a ride – at work *or* at home – from a meditative point of view it is also important to acknowledge the source of the anger we can sometimes feel in life. In this instance, it was the way in which I'd been spoken to that ignited the anger. But from there on in, it was entirely my own work. That doesn't defend the attitude of the monk, but allowed me to take responsibility for the part I played in the continuation of that anger. Focusing on the wet grass and my sore back were just ways of keeping the fire burning, rather than letting go of the anger. On another day and in a different mood, I would probably not have been too bothered about either. But on this day I'm quite sure that even if somebody had told me I'd won the Lottery (not that we played in the monastery of course), I would have still found a way to continue feeling angry. Letting go of such strong emotions is not always easy.

It took about an hour for the mind to settle down. Strangely enough it seemed to happen at the same time that I started concentrating less on the thoughts and more on the task at hand. And while I appreciate cutting the lawn with a pair of scissors will not be everyone's cup of tea, there was actually something very soothing about the process after a while. In fact, it became a meditation of its own. I figured there was no point in rushing, it didn't really matter how many days it took me. And in being a bit of a perfectionist, there was something actually quite nice about trying to get it 'just right', and the less I indulged the thoughts, the less momentum anger had. As the anger decreased, so I could see more clearly what was happening in the mind. I started to get some perspective on things, which led to the mind becoming even more calm. It became cyclical: calm leading to clarity leading to calm leading to clarity. Before long I was laughing at myself, wondering what my friends would think if they could only see me now. Not for the first time I might add. Most importantly though, the mind had now settled and I no longer felt angry.

The same street

We often underestimate the value of clarity – I know I always used to. I'd got so used to living with a confused mind that I didn't know whether I had clarity or not (clearly I didn't). I kept making the same mistakes – no matter how many times the same situation arose in life, I reacted to it in the same way. I'd blindly stumble into situations, not really knowing how I got there, not really knowing how to change things, and causing myself and others a lot of problems in the process. I remember discussing this with a Tibetan teacher in Nepal, very early on when I'd just started to meditate. I asked him how, given all the meditation I was doing at the time, I was still making many of the same mistakes.

'Imagine every day you have to walk to work,' he began. 'You walk down the same street, see the same houses, the same people, every day.' I pictured the scene. I'd had several jobs like that in the past, so it didn't require much imagination. 'Towards the end of this street there is a very big hole. Perhaps the workmen have been digging it up to repair the pipes or something, but the hole is very deep and because the workmen have been drinking too much tea, or spent too much time talking, this hole always seems to be there.' He stopped and laughed at the image. 'So,' he went on, 'even though you know this big hole is there, every day you go down the same street and walk straight into the hole. You don't mean to do it, it's just that you've got so used to following that particular path, that course of action, that you do it without even thinking.' Although I couldn't relate to this on an external level (why would I keep walking into the same hole every day?), it certainly chimed with my internal world. I don't know about you, but for me it perfectly mirrored how I'd always walk into the same old emotional traps and mental confusion.

'Now,' he said, 'when you start to meditate it's like you wake up and become more aware of what's going on around you. When you walk down the street, you see the big hole in front of you.' 'But that's the thing,' I replied, 'I've been meditating a lot and although sometimes I see the hole, there's nothing I can do to stop myself falling down it every time.' He smiled. 'Exactly,' he said, 'at first you just see the hole, but the habit of walking down that part of the street is so strong that you can't help but walk straight into it. You know it's madness, you know that it's going to hurt, but you just can't help yourself!' By this point he was laughing out loud. Despite my anguish, I had to admit that there was something pretty funny about this image. He continued, 'This is just how it is with your mind. You see these pitfalls, but the habit is so strong you can't help yourself from falling. But,' he said, pausing dramatically, 'if you *continue* meditating, you'll begin to see the hole much earlier and be able to take some evasive action. At first you may try to go around the edge and fall in anyway. This is part of the process. But eventually, with practice, you'll see it with such clarity that you'll simply walk around it and continue on your way. This way you'll arrive at work feeling very fresh.' He chuckled again. 'And then one day, you might have so much clarity, you might be so awake, that you realise that there was never a hole there in the first place, but that's a lesson for another time.'

Over the years I've found this story useful to reflect on. In many ways it sums up the process of meditation. And it's just that, a process. Just because you sit for a few minutes each day doesn't mean that you will immediately master the mind and no longer fall prey to your old habits. That's not to say you won't sometimes experience those 'lightbulb' moments, when you realise what it is you've been doing. But the process will likely be a gradual one, where each day you see the hole a little earlier, with a little more clarity. In doing so, you'll manage to avoid many of the habitual reactions that stress you out. This is what it means to have awareness, to see the mind with absolute clarity.

The theatre

Pretty much everything we do in life is judged in terms of good or bad, better or worse. But when it comes to meditation there's no such thing as good or bad, and there's a good reason for this. Another way of describing meditation is to use the word 'awareness'. So, if you're unaware, then you are not meditating *badly*, you're not meditating *at all*! It doesn't matter whether you're aware of lots of thoughts or of no thoughts. Nor does it matter whether you're aware of pleasant feelings or unpleasant feelings. The skill is simply to be aware, that's all. One teacher of mine used to repeat this like a mantra. He'd say, 'If you're distracted, then it's not meditation. Only if you're undistracted is it meditation. There's no such thing as good and bad meditation, there is only distracted or undistracted, aware or unaware.' In fact, he used to liken it to going to the theatre.

Imagine you're watching a play of several acts. Your only role is to sit back, relax and watch as the story unfolds. It's not your job to direct the performance, neither is it your job to get up on stage and start interfering with the story being told. It might be a story of love and romance, of action and bravado, or of mystery and intrigue. Or it might have elements of them all. The show might be fast moving and leave you breathless, or it might move at a very sedate pace, leaving you relaxed and at ease. The thing is that no matter what happens, your only job is to watch the play unfold. To begin with this might be quite easy, but maybe the story's slow moving and you start to get restless. Perhaps you look around for other things to entertain you, or think about things you need to do the next day. At this point in time, you're completely unaware of what's happening on the stage. This is a common tendency when learning to meditate, so don't be hard on yourself. Besides, the moment you realise that your mind has drifted off, you are immediately back with the play and following the story again.

Sometimes the story might be particularly unpleasant. In these moments it's very difficult not to lose yourself in the play. Perhaps you even start thinking for the actors on stage. You may feel so involved in these moments that you find it hard to resist the temptation to call out, or jump to the actors' defence. Or it might be an uplifting tale that brings about a pleasant and comforting feeling inside. In these moments you might see something in the actor or actress that you've always wanted for yourself in life. Or maybe you're reminded of an old relationship and the mind drifts off to memories past. Perhaps you even feel so inspired by the story that you sit there planning how best to ask out that person you've been wanting to ask out for the last five years.

When you sit to meditate it's a little like watching this play. The images and voices are not *you*, in the same way that the play or the film is not *you*. It's an unfolding story that you're watching, observing and witnessing. This is what it means to be aware. Your own story, as in your own life, will still require direction and a sense of engagement, but when sitting to observe the mind during your meditation, taking a seat in the audience is by far the best way of watching. And it's through developing that ability of passive observation that you get to experience the clarity and confidence to make decisions, make changes and live life more fully. Think back to the blue sky, this space that has always been there. Awareness is not something you need to create, as it's always present. We just need to remember not to forget.

The imaginary lovers

When I was training as a novice monk, I stayed in several monasteries that were generally closed to the public, but that once in a while opened their doors so that lay-people could come and do a one-week meditation retreat. The men would stay in the monks' quarters and the women would live with the nuns. Each day they'd come together for a number of meditation sessions. These retreats were always conducted in silence, to offer the participants as few distractions as possible. For some people this really helped, while for others it was torture to go a whole week without talking. Every afternoon the participants would visit the respective monks and nuns and report back on how their meditation was going. Over the years the monks and the nuns started to recognise a pattern of behaviour that seemed to repeat itself. In the moments when the men and women would come together, eyes would inevitably wander, sometimes catching another pair of wandering eyes in the process. This would usually happen early on in the week. Little did the pair realise at the time the significance of this fleeting glance. The man would go back to his room and sit to meditate. Within seconds he'd be thinking about this woman, talking to himself in the process. 'She definitely looked at me. I think I might be in there. And this is perfect, she's interested in meditation, so we'd have loads in common. Right, as soon as we're allowed to talk I'll ask her out.' Already he'd be looking forward to the next meeting of eyes.

Meanwhile, over in the nuns' quarters, the woman would be thinking, 'I wonder if he saw me? Did he like me? It would be so nice to be in a relationship with someone who's sensitive enough to take care of his own mind.' Not even ten minutes has passed and yet already the 'R' word has popped up in the internal conversation! This pattern would continue throughout the week, the pair stealing glances once in a while and then feeding off their projection of those glances the rest of the time. We've all done it, right? By the end of the week, it's no exaggeration to say that some couples had taken that chain of thought so far, that not only had they dated in their minds, but they'd got married, consummated the marriage, had children, and spent time thinking where they might retire to. Some had even got divorced! Even though it was their own story that they were creating, they had still chosen to build in some pain and anguish. Yet they'd never even spoken to the other person. This shows how easy it is to get caught up in all the little stories, the dramas, the hopes and the fears of the mind.

Part of the reason that we get so easily drawn into these stories is that we're so used to *doing* something, being *involved* in something, that it can feel a bit boring to just sit and watch the mind, especially if the thoughts are mundane. We create these stories in an attempt to make things interesting, to get away from the boredom. But have you ever stayed with boredom long enough to look at what it is? Is it simply a thought or a feeling of wanting to be somewhere else, of doing something different? And if so, then why treat that thought or feeling any differently from all the others you observe in the mind? As you know, just because we experience a thought doesn't mean we have to react to it, or act upon it. We'd be in pretty big trouble if we always did. We actually have the ability not to take thoughts too seriously. It's just that we've created boundaries for when we should start to take them seriously. Think back to a time when you might have had a thought that was so extreme you laughed at it. In that moment, you saw it for what it was, a crazy thought, no more than that. And so you didn't give it too much importance and probably let it go. So we have this ability within us, it's just getting used to the feeling of taking up the position of an observer on a more regular basis.

The screaming man

I remember hearing a funny story of a man who went to visit a Buddhist monastery in the UK. He was keen to try meditation and had heard that it was possible to join the monks and nuns in the temple for one of the sessions during the day. So, after making some enquiries, he was shown to the temple doors and left to go and find a seat. All of the monks and nuns were sitting at the front of the room and all of the lay-people were sitting behind them. Not wanting to be right at the back, he walked a little further into the middle of the room. Almost immediately a loud gong sounded which, looking around at the other people in the hall, appeared to the man to signify the beginning of the meditation session. Having shuffled around a little to try and get comfortable (he wasn't used to sitting on the floor), he closed his eyes and began. He knew he was supposed to focus on his breath, and he thought he was supposed to have an empty mind, but he had no idea how he was going to make that happen. In fact, this was much like me when I first started meditation.

To begin with he sat very still and tried diligently to follow the breath. But no matter how hard he tried, his mind kept wandering off and he became increasingly anxious, impatient and frustrated. After a while he was so caught up in these thoughts that he'd unintentionally abandoned any idea of focusing on the breath at all. Instead he was feeding the frustration with even more thoughts. 'This meditation doesn't work at all. I feel terrible. I felt fine when I came in and now I feel awful, what's the point in that? I'm rubbish at this. Typical, I'm rubbish at everything. Can't one thing in my life go right for a change? Can't I even just have one hour to sit and enjoy the silence? How much longer is this going to go on? It feels like we've been sitting here for ever. I thought they said it would only last an hour. This feels more like two hours!' He continued to think in this way, using one thought to fuel the next, increasing the intensity of his frustration and making it more and more difficult to sit there in the process.

Eventually he reached breaking point. He was no longer conscious of that separation between audience and stage. He was now (metaphorically speaking) up out of his seat, running around the stage and creating mayhem in his wake. He had 'become' his thoughts. He was desperate, unable to contain himself for a moment longer. Without even being conscious of doing so, he jumped up from his seat in the middle of the temple and screamed out at the top of his voice, 'I can't fucking do this any more.' In a twist of cruel irony this was followed immediately by the gong, signifying the end of the hour and the end of the session.

There are several valuable lessons here, each as important as the next. First, if you're going to learn a new skill you need the right instructions. It's no use thinking, 'Oh well, how hard can it be to just sit there and watch your own mind?', because, as the man in the story demonstrated, if you don't know the right way of watching the mind, then it can be very difficult indeed. The second is that if you're going to learn how to meditate, then start slowly. There's nothing wrong with taking just ten minutes to begin with. In fact, this is a long time if you've never done anything like this before. In the same way that the body needs to be trained to run marathons, so the mind needs to be trained to sit for longer periods of time. The story also illustrates the danger of waiting for the meditation to finish. It's a common experience and it's almost as though we think that by simply sitting there and not moving, we're meditating, no matter what we're doing with the mind. But this underlying sense of expectation, of waiting for something to happen, is a mind that is looking to the future, as opposed to a mind resting in the present. Think about it, how can there ever be a sense of ease resting in the present moment if the mind is hurriedly trying to get to a space and time in the future?

Take10 – introduction

Having spent some time looking at how best to approach meditation (and how to avoid some of the most common mistakes), it seems only fitting to turn our attention to the technique itself. Some aspects of this ten-minute exercise will appear quite familiar, as they're similar to the short two-minute exercises you've already done. Although by now you might be itching to get started, I'd strongly recommend that you read the following section in full before you sit down to do Take10. While the first page may appear to have all the necessary information, it is in fact just a summary – a useful list of the key points to remember. You might like to have this near you the first few times you do the meditation, just in case you forget the order of things. But remember you can also access the guided version by visiting the website at www.getsome-headspace.com/headspace-book/get-some-headspace.

What follows the summary is a more detailed explanation of the four sections. The first section is just taking care of the practicalities and getting yourself ready. The next section is about taming that wild horse, bringing the mind to a natural and comfortable place of rest. Following that is a short section where you'll be focusing on the rising and falling movement of the breath and then freeing your mind altogether while you just sit back and enjoy the silence. Finally, there is the part when you make the conscious effort to carry that sense of presence and awareness into your everyday life and into the relationships with people around you.

Take10 – summary

Getting ready:
1 Find a place to sit down comfortably, keeping a straight back.
2 Ensure you'll be left undisturbed during your meditation (switch off your mobile).
3 Set the timer for 10 minutes.

Checking-in:
1 Take 5 deep breaths, breathing in through the nose and out through the mouth and then gently close your eyes.
2 Focus on the physical sensation of the body on the chair and the feet on the floor.
3 Scan down through the body and notice which parts feel comfortable and relaxed, and which parts feel uncomfortable and tense.
4 Notice how you're feeling – i.e. what sort of mood you're in right now.

Focusing the mind:
1 Notice where you feel the rising and falling sensation of the breath most strongly.
2 Notice how each breath feels, the rhythm of it – whether it's long or short, deep or shallow, rough or smooth.
3 Gently count the breaths as you focus on the rising and falling sensation – 1 with the rise and 2 with the fall, upwards to a count of 10.
4 Repeat this cycle between 5 and 10 times, or for as long as you have time available.

Finishing-off:
1 Let go of any focus at all, allowing the mind to be as busy or as still as it wants to be for about 20 seconds.
2 Bring the mind back to the sensation of the body on the chair and the feet on the floor.
3 Gently open your eyes and stand up when you feel ready.

Take10 – explained

Getting ready
This section is all about preparing yourself for meditation in the right way. You'd be amazed at how many people rush around like crazy and then quickly sit down and close their eyes, waiting for the mind to be quiet. How's that ever going to work? If you're busy in your mind beforehand, then it will take that much longer for the mind to quieten when you sit to meditate.

If you can, start to slow down five or ten minutes beforehand so that you begin the exercise in the right frame of mind. Make sure you've set the timer if you're using one and that you'll be left undisturbed for the next ten minutes. While it's best to learn meditation sitting upright in a chair, you may feel that you'd rather do it lying down. This may sound more appealing, but it's a lot more difficult to get the right balance of focus and relaxation when you do it lying down and you may well find yourself drifting off into sleep. If you *do* choose this option, make sure you lie on a firm surface with the arms and legs out straight. You might also like to place a pillow under the knees to take the pressure off your lower back.

Checking-in

This next phase is about bringing the body and mind together. Think how often your body is doing one thing and yet your mind is off doing something else. Perhaps you're walking down the street, but your mind is already at home, planning the dinner or wondering what's on television. It's actually very rare that the body and mind arc together at the same place and the same time. So this is an opportunity to settle into your environment, to be consciously aware of what you're doing and where you are.

Ideally, 'checking-in' should take about five minutes to begin with. As you get more familiar with the process and more skilled, then you may find it doesn't take quite so long, but it's important not to rush this part. Some people approach checking-in with the idea that it's just an optional preparation and not part of the actual exercise. They might think, 'Right, let's get this bit out of the way so I can get on to the real stuff, focusing on my breath and slowing down this crazy mind.' But the mind doesn't work in this way. Think back to the wild horse analogy and that idea of giving it all the space it needs to begin with, rather than trying to pin it down immediately in one place. Checking-in is all about bringing the horse into a natural place of rest.

Begin with the eyes open. Not staring at one particular thing, but rather looking forwards with a very soft gaze, aware of your peripheral vision too – above, below, and to either side. Then take five deep breaths, breathing in through the nose and out through the mouth. As you breathe in, really try to get a sense of the lungs filling with air and the chest expanding. And as you breathe out, just let the breath go. You don't need to forcefully exhale, but just let the breath go and imagine that you're letting go of any tension or stress you might have been holding on to. As you breathe out for the fifth time, you can gently close your eyelids. You can then allow the breath to return to its own natural rhythm, in and out of the nose.

In closing the eyes you'll immediately become more aware of physical sensations and, in particular, the way in which you're sitting. Are the shoulders slumped forward? Are the hands and arms being fully supported by the legs? This is a good opportunity to adjust these things before you get too far into the exercise. Next, bring your attention to the physical sensation of the chair beneath you and the weight of the body pressing down on it. This is the feeling of the contact between your body and the chair. Notice whether the weight falls evenly down through the middle of the body or whether you feel it pressing down a little more to one side. Now do exactly the same with the feet, simply noticing the sensation between the soles of the feet and the floor. Where is the point of contact strongest? Is it on the heel, the toe, the inside or the outside of the foot? Pause here for just long enough to be clear about this feeling. And then, lastly, repeat this process with the hands and the arms. Feel the weight of gravity, the weight of the arms being supported by the legs, and the contact of the hands on the legs. You don't have to *do* anything about it, being aware of it is enough. Simply shift your attention to each sensation and remember to apply a sense of gentle curiosity.

As you're doing this there will undoubtedly be lots of thoughts popping up in the mind. This is perfectly normal and you don't need to do anything to try to change it. They're just thoughts. Think back to the road analogy. The idea is not to try and stop the thoughts, but rather to step back and just allow them to come and go with your full awareness. Besides, at this point we're paying attention to the physical sensations rather than any thoughts or emotions, so you can just allow those to come and go in the background.

Take a moment to notice any sounds. These might be very close to you, or perhaps in another room, or even outside the building. It might be the sound of cars passing by, people talking, an air-conditioning unit. It doesn't matter what the sounds are, you can just witness them coming and going. Sometimes you might catch yourself getting 'involved' in a sound, perhaps tuning into a conversation. This is quite normal, and in fact as soon as you realise you've got caught up in one particular sound, then you will start to notice all the other little sounds again. If you live in a busy city, external sounds are often seen as a kind of obstacle to meditation, something that gets in the way of a quiet mind. But it doesn't have to be that way. To begin with, it's preferable if you can sit in a quiet room, but by making a conscious effort to acknowledge the sounds, rather than resist them, something very interesting begins to happen. You can repeat this process with your other senses if you like, just briefly noticing any strong smells, or even tastes you may have in your mouth. In this way the mind is fully engaged with the physical senses.

The next thing to do is to build up a picture of how the body *feels*. Start by getting a general sense of any areas of tension or relaxation. We're not trying to change any of the feelings at this point, but rather building up a picture. This first scan might take just 10 seconds or so. It's as if you were surveying a house from the outside only. But then you need to go into the house and get a bit more detail about the condition of the building. So, in order to do this, next take a good thirty seconds or so to scan down through the body (from the top of the head, down to the toes), noticing how the different parts of the body feel. What feels comfortable and what feels uncomfortable? Where are the areas of tension and where are the areas of relaxation? As you're doing this it's tempting to zoom in and focus only on the areas of tension. In fact, sometimes it might even feel as though there is nothing *but* tension! But try as much as possible to work systematically, scanning down the body, noticing both comfort and discomfort. Don't forget to notice the fingers, the toes and the ears. How do they feel?

As you're scanning you may become more aware of your thoughts and feelings, even though you're not specifically focusing on them. Just allow these to come and go in the background. As soon as you realise that you've been distracted, that the mind has wandered off, just gently bring your attention back to the body scan, back to the place you left off from. This is normal and will probably happen many, many times, so it's nothing to worry about. If you do notice a particularly strong emotional quality to the mind, then it can be useful simply to acknowledge it.

We're usually so caught up in our thoughts, so busy with the activities of the day, that we're often unaware of how we're feeling emotionally. This may not sound that important, but if you're aware of how you feel then you're in a position to respond to that feeling. Whereas if you are unaware, you will in all likelihood find yourself reacting impulsively at some stage during the day. We've all observed it – the mild-mannered businessman or housewife, seemingly well adjusted, standing calmly in line at the supermarket, and then suddenly losing it. Perhaps they get bumped by a trolley, or maybe their card is declined at the till, things that on another day they would brush off, but because of that underlying feeling, it all boils over and ends up in some kind of outburst.

People often say they haven't got a clue how they feel and that's OK too. Being aware that you haven't got a clue is still being aware, and the more times you repeat the process of checking-in, the more you'll become aware of an underlying feeling or mood. The emotional feelings are treated no differently to the physical sensations in this particular exercise. It doesn't matter whether it's an emotion that you perceive as pleasant or unpleasant, comfortable or uncomfortable. For the purpose of this exercise, no analysis or judgment is required whatsoever. It's enough simply to notice the feeling, to acknowledge it and be aware of it.

Finally, while it's not absolutely necessary, you might also find it useful to briefly (I'm talking five to ten seconds here) acknowledge any particular issues that you might have going on in your life. It might be that you're feeling excited about an upcoming event, or perhaps feeling anxious about a meeting you've just had. Perhaps you're feeling angry about a conversation you had with someone, or feeling happy about some praise you just received. Whatever it is, acknowledge it and be aware that it's around. If it's been taking up a lot of space in your mind recently, then it's almost inevitable that it will pop up during the exercise at some stage. By being clear about this at the very beginning, then you are setting up a framework in which those thoughts can arise and fall away again, without getting sucked back into thinking about them.

As I say, this entire process of checking-in should take about five minutes to begin with, and if you only have five minutes to spare, then only do this part of the exercise – *that's* how important it is. Without going through this process, there's very little benefit to jumping ahead and focusing on the breath. So make sure you take your time with this section. Although checking-in is part of the meditation itself you can make good use of it in lots of other situations too. You can use it sitting on the bus, at your desk, or even standing in a queue. You might like to make the deep breaths a little more subtle, and if you are standing up then you will probably want to avoid closing your eyes. But otherwise you can do the exercise in the same way and still get to experience that same sense of ease in the mind.

Focusing on the breath

Once we've brought the 'horse' to a natural place of rest, it may continue to fidget a little, or start to get bored. So we need to give it something to focus on. As I've said, the breath is one of the easiest and most flexible of objects to use, so for the purpose of this exercise the breath will be the primary focus.

Begin by taking just a few moments (about thirty seconds) to observe the breath, in particular the rising and falling sensation that is created as the breath passes in and out of the body. At first, simply notice where in the body you feel that sensation most strongly. It might be in the abdomen, around the diaphragm, in the chest, or even in the shoulders. No matter where you feel it most clearly, just take a moment to notice the physical sensation of the breath rising and falling in that way. If the breath is very shallow and hard to detect, you might find it helpful, and even reas-suring, to place your hand lightly on the abdomen over the area just below the belly-button. You can quite easily trace the rise and fall of the stomach as your hand moves back and forth. You can then return the hand to its initial position, resting in the lap, before continuing the exercise.

Because the breath and mind are so intimately connected, it's possible that you might not be happy with the location of the breath. That may well sound very strange to some of you, but it's actually a very common phenomena. People often complain that they are not 'breathing properly', that they can only feel the move-ment in their chest. And yet, they say, they've read books and been to yoga classes where they've been instructed to take big deep breaths from the stomach. At first glance this makes sense, we natu-rally associate the times when we've been very relaxed, perhaps feeling sleepy on the sofa, or lying in the bath, with long, slow breaths, seemingly coming from the stomach. Equally, we associate times of anxiety or worry with short, shallow breaths, seemingly coming from the area of the chest. If you sit down and experience the feelings similar to that anxious type of breathing, then it's natural that you might think you're doing something wrong. But you're actually doing nothing wrong at all. Remember, there is only aware and unaware, undistracted and distracted – there is no such thing as wrong breathing or bad breathing in the context of this exercise. Of course, there are specific breathing exercises that might be part of yoga or some other tradition, but that's not where we're going with this exercise.

If you've made it to this point in your life and are reading this book right now, then I'm assuming you've breathed perfectly well up until this point. In fact, I would guess that unless you've done previous exercises with relaxation or perhaps yoga, most of the time you won't even have been aware of how you're breathing. The breath is autonomous, it doesn't require our control in order to function. Left alone to its own natural intelligence, the breath generally functions quite comfortably. So, rather than trying to exert your control (notice a theme building up anywhere here?), allow the body to do its own thing. It will regulate itself in its own time and its own way. Sometimes it might appear more obvious in one place and then shift as you're watching it. At other times it will rest quite comfortably in the one place the entire time, whether that's the stomach, chest or someplace in-between. Your only job here is to notice, to observe, and to be aware of what the body is doing naturally.

So without any effort to try and change the location of the breath, rest your attention on that physical movement, that rising and falling sensation. As you're doing this, you can slowly begin to notice the rhythm of the breath. How does the breath feel in the body? Is it fast or is it slow? Take a good few seconds before you try and answer. Are the breaths deep or are they shallow? You can also notice whether the breath feels rough or smooth, tight or spacious, and warm or cool. These may sound like strange questions, but they follow that same idea of applying a gentle curiosity to your meditation. This process should only take about thirty seconds.

Having got a good sense of how those sensations feel in the body, now focus on the breath as it comes and goes each time. The easiest way of doing this is to count the breaths (silently to yourself) as they pass. As you feel the rising sensation count 1, and as you feel the falling sensation count 2. Keep counting in this way to the count of 10. When you get to 10, return to 1 and repeat the exercise. It sounds easier than it is. If you're anything like me when I started, you'll find that you count to 3 or 4 each time before your mind will wander off to something more interesting. Alternatively, you may suddenly find yourself counting 62, 63, 64 . . . and realise that you forgot to stop at 10. Both are very common and part of the process of learning meditation.

In the moment you realise that you've been distracted, that the mind has wandered off, you're no longer distracted. So all you need to do is gently bring the attention back to the physical sensation of the breath and continue to count. If you can remember the number you were on then just pick it up from there and, if not, simply start again at 1. There are no prizes for making it to 10 (I'm sorry to say) and so it doesn't matter whether you start again at 1 or not. In fact, it can be quite funny in how difficult it is to make it to 10 each time, and it's OK to laugh if you feel like laughing. For some reason meditation can look very serious and it can be tempting to start treating it like 'serious work'. But the more you can bring a sense of humour to it, a sense of play, the easier and more enjoyable you'll find it.

Continue to count in this way until the timer you've set lets you know that it's the end of the session. But don't jump up from your chair just yet. There is still one very important part left to do.

Finishing-off

This part is often overlooked and yet it's one of the most important aspects of the exercise. When you've come to the end of the counting, just let your mind be completely free. Don't try to control it in any way. This means not focusing on the breath, not focusing on counting, or anything else at all. If your mind wants to be busy, let it be busy. If it wants to be quiet and there are no thoughts at all, let it be quiet. It requires no effort, no sense of control or censorship of any kind at all, just letting the mind be completely free. Does that sound like a wonderful or a frightening proposition I wonder. Either way, just let your mind loose for about ten or twenty seconds before bringing the meditation to a close. Sometimes when you do this you may notice that the thoughts are actually less than when you were trying to focus on the breath. 'How can that be?' you may well ask. If you think back to the example of the stallion that hasn't yet been broken in, he's often more comfortable and more at ease when he has a bit of space, when he tends not to cause so much trouble. But when he's tied up a bit too tightly, then he tends to kick a little. So if you're able to bring some of this spacious quality into the part of the technique where you focus on the breath, then you will really start to see a lot more benefit from the meditation.

Having let the mind roam free for that short while, slowly bring the attention back to the physical sensations in the body. This means bringing the mind into the physical senses. Notice once again the firm contact between the body and the chair beneath you, between the soles of the feet and the floor, and between the hands and the legs. Take a moment to notice any sounds, any strong smells, or tastes, slowly grounding yourself through contact and awareness with each of the senses. This has the effect of bringing you fully back into the environment you're sitting in. Gently open the eyes first and take a moment to readjust, to refocus, and be aware of the space around you. Then, with the intention to carry that sense of awareness and presence into the next part of your day, slowly get up from the chair. Be clear where you're going next and what you're about to do, as this will help to maintain that sense of aware-ness. Maybe it's going to the kitchen to make a cup of tea, or perhaps it's going back to the office to sit at your computer. It doesn't matter what it is, what matters is being clear enough in your own mind that you're able to continue experiencing each moment, one after the next, with your full awareness.

What the research shows

1 Meditation changes the shape of your brain

Researchers from the University of Montreal investigated the difference in brain responses of meditators and non-meditators when they experienced pain. The scientists found that the areas of the brain which regulate pain and emotion were significantly thicker in meditators compared to non-meditators. This is important, because the thicker the region, the lower the pain sensitivity. This potential for change in the brain is known as neuroplasticity. It means that when you sit to meditate, not only are you changing your perspective, but you could also be changing the physical structure of the brain.

2 Mindfulness offers an enhanced quality of life

In a randomized control study, researchers found that a mindfulness-based approach was more effective than medication in preventing the relapse of depression. Now clearly there are some situations when medication is required, but this study makes for interesting reading. In just six months, 75% of the mindfulness practitioners completely discontinued their medication. The researchers also found that they were less likely to relapse. Not only that, but they experienced an 'enhanced quality of life' compared to those on medication.

3 Meditation can help to clear your skin

A Professor of Medicine at the University of Massachusetts Medical School undertook a study to see if meditation could influence the healing of psoriasis, a treatable skin condition that has a strong relationship with psychological stress. With clear implications for other stress-related skin conditions, they found that the meditators' skin cleared at about four times the rate of the non-meditators' skin.

4 Mindfulness relieves anxiety and depression

In a comprehensive analysis of thirty-nine different studies, researchers from Boston University examined how effective mindfulness had been in treating anxiety and depression in patients suffering from other illness. They found that meditation had a significant effect on the symptoms across a wide range of health disorders. The researchers concluded the benefits are so far-reaching because meditators learn how to work better with difficulties in general, and so therefore experience less stress in life.

5 Meditation may help improve your chances of conceiving

A recent study from Oxford University, investigating the impact of stress on 274 healthy women aged between eighteen and forty, found that stress can reduce the chances of women conceiving. The head of the research team suggested that techniques such as meditation could be instrumental in combating this decline in fertility.

The Integration

I'd always assumed that meditation was done sitting down with your eyes closed. So it was quite a shock when I turned up at one of my very first monasteries and was introduced not only to the cross-legged seated variety of meditation, but also to walking and standing techniques and even meditation done lying down. Now if you're anything like me, you'll already be thinking, 'Oh yeah, the lying-down meditation's the one for me!' – though I'm sorry to say it doesn't really work like that. Although you can still get a lot of benefit from lying down to meditate, your practice will be that much stronger if you can learn to do it sitting upright in a chair. These four types of meditation posture were not there to give us a choice as to how we'd like to meditate, but were an introduction to mindfulness. If you think back to the introduction, mindfulness simply means to be present, undistracted, in the moment, as opposed to lost in thought and caught up in the emotions. By learning how to *meditate* in all four postures (if you think about it, we're always in one of them, if not in transition from one to the next), we were at the same time being taught how to be *mindful* in all four postures.

It may be tempting to think, 'Yeah, but I bet the seated meditation is when the magic really starts to happen.' So to give you some idea of how important these other postures are considered in the overall training of meditation, take the example of the daily schedule at this particular monastery.

We got up at 2.45 a.m. and started meditation at 3 a.m. We had break-fast at 5 a.m. and lunch at 11 a.m. and then one short tea-break in the afternoon. (In the tradition of this monastery, and indeed most other Buddhist monasteries, we didn't eat after noon, so there was no break for dinner in the evening.) We finally went to bed at around 11 p.m. Now you've probably already done the maths, but this ensured a total of about eighteen hours of formal meditation practice every day. Of these eighteen hours, *half* were dedicated to walking/standing meditation, and the other half to sitting meditation, the sessions alter-nating one after the next. *That's* how important they're considered.

As for the horizontal meditation, alas, that was taught purely for the benefit of falling asleep (or if we were too unwell to meditate sitting upright). The idea of falling asleep in this way is that a certain amount of awareness can be maintained throughout the night if you're lying in the correct position and maintain the right attitude of mind. In fact, there was such an emphasis placed on this, that the first question the teacher would ask me each day was 'Did you awake on the in-breath or the out-breath this morning?' It was a question to which at first I frequently shrugged my shoul-ders by means of a reply. Try it, it's not nearly as easy as it sounds. With a bit of practice, though, you'd be surprised how quickly you can become aware of these details.

I remember vividly the first moment I realised the full implica-tion of being mindful of the body in this way. As is often the way with meditation, it wasn't during the formal practice but later on when I was walking along the road. Up until then I'd understood the concept of mindfulness, but hadn't really appreciated the full potential of it. I was walking down the road, in the same way as you would normally, but applying the instructions for walking meditation (which you'll find later in this book), when all of a sudden it hit me that in being 100 per cent present with the process of walking, with the physical sensation itself, I wasn't experiencing any thoughts. If I was truly present with one thing, then I couldn't be present with another at the same time. So, without trying to ignore or resist thoughts, they were naturally decreasing on their own as I focused my mind elsewhere.

At first glance this discovery may not sound all that extraordinary to you. In fact, it may sound quite obvious. But if it were that obvious, then surely we'd do it all the time, because it's only when we're caught up in all the thoughts that we get stressed. So for me it was the realisation that the mind can only be in one place at one time. Sure, sometimes it moves so quickly from one thing to the next that it gives the impression of being in more than one place at one time, but that's just an illusion. The reality in that situation was that by placing 100 per cent of my attention on the physical sensation of walking, the mind was no longer lost in thought. I became quite excited about this idea, with visions of how wonderful my new life would be, always living in the present, never distracted by thinking. In fact, I got so carried away with it that within just a couple of minutes I'd lost all sense of awareness and was completely lost in thought again! As I said before, I think it's best to think of insight as drips of water filling a bucket, rather than any great thunderbolt that might transform your life instantaneously.

Mindfulness in action

Although it requires consistent effort to be mindful, just like the meditation technique, it's an *effortless* type of effort that's needed. The effort is simply remembering to notice when you've been caught up in thoughts or feelings and, in that moment, redirecting your attention to a particular point of focus. It doesn't matter whether the point of focus is the taste of the food that you're eating, the movement of your arm as you open and close a door, the weight of your body pressing against a chair beneath you, the sensation of water against your skin as you're taking a shower, the sound of your heart beating as you exercise, the physical sensation of touch between you and your baby, the smell of toothpaste as you're brushing your teeth, or even the simple act of drinking a glass of water. Awareness can be applied to every little thing you do – no exceptions. It can be applied to both passive and dynamic activities, indoors and outdoors, at work and at play, and alone or with others.

If you're new to mindfulness then at first this may sound confusing. I regularly get asked by people whether that means they now have to walk down the street with their eyes closed while watching their breath. First of all, please don't! You'll probably walk out in front of a car. Second, we're now talking about general mindfulness rather than a specific meditation, so there's no need to close your eyes and no need to focus on the breath. Again, mindfulness means to be present, aware of what you're doing and where you are. You don't have to do anything differently from how you would normally do it. The only thing you need to do is be aware. And the easiest way of doing that is to have a point of focus. Every time you realise the mind has wandered off, you simply bring your attention back to that original focal point.

One of my favourite examples is brushing the teeth. It's a familiar activity, with a very obvious focal point and, as it's likely to last no more than a few minutes, there's every chance that you'll be able to maintain a sense of awareness throughout. Of course, this is in contrast to how most people would normally brush their teeth, which is as quickly as possible while thinking about what to do next. The difference between the two scenarios needs to be experienced to be fully understood. Try it, see how it feels. You'll probably find it easiest to be aware of one of the physical senses and use that as your focal point. So it might be the sound of the brush against the teeth, or the physical sensation of the arm moving back and forwards, or the taste or the smell of the toothpaste. By focusing on just one of these objects at a time, the mind will start to feel a little more calm. And in that calmness there's every possibility that you might notice the tendency to drift off into thought, or to hurry to get on to the next thing. Or you might notice that you apply too much or too little effort to the brushing process. You may even notice a feeling of boredom. But all these observations will prove useful in their own way, because they will show you your mind as it really is. Having this increased awareness is the difference between having a stable, calm and focused mind, or a mind that feels out of control. Take the example of drinking a glass of water. Rather than just 'necking it' as quickly as possible, take the time to notice the experience. Seriously, when was the last time you actually *tasted* a glass of water? As you pick up the glass you can be aware of the temperature and texture of the glass. You can be aware of the movement of the hand towards the mouth. You can be aware of the taste and texture of the water as it enters the mouth. If you're really listening to the body you can even follow the water as it goes down the throat towards the stomach. And if you notice the mind has wandered off at any one of these stages, it's simply a matter of bringing the attention back to the process of drinking the water.

What you'll notice when you start to apply this approach to situations is that it has a very soothing effect on the mind. Not only are you present to experience everything you do (quite literally living life to the full), but it also feels very calming. And with calm comes clarity. You begin to see how and why you think and feel the way you do. You start to notice the patterns and tendencies of the mind. And what this does is to give you back the choice of how you live your life. Rather than being swept away by undermining or unproductive thoughts and emotions, you can respond in the way you'd actually like to.

Another common question is how does this work if other people are present. Is it not rude to be focusing on these things if you are in the company of others? This one always makes me laugh, because it suggests that normally we're so focused on the words, feelings and sensitivities of others that we couldn't possibly have time to focus on anything else. Needless to say, this is rarely the case. We're often so distracted by our own thoughts that we don't even really hear what the other person is saying. Let's say you're walking down the street talking with a friend. Although walking is a relatively autonomous act, you will still have to apply a certain amount of awareness to avoid bumping into other people, walking in front of traffic and so on. Between those moments of awareness, your attention can easily switch to listening and engaging with your friend. This doesn't mean you are giving them any less attention than you would usually, it simply means your attention is switching from one thing to the next as required – in this case from an awareness of your physical surroundings to an awareness of listening and talking to your friend. The awareness of passing thoughts and feelings will not be as refined as you would experience when sitting to do your meditation practice – at least not at first anyway, but the important thing is to apply the *intention* of awareness. The more often you do this the easier and more refined it will become. By being mindful, it actually puts you 'back in the room' with the other person, or people. One woman who came to the clinic commented on how by using it with her baby, she now felt as if she was actually spending time with him. She'd said that before, even though she was with him, her mind was always elsewhere. But by being more mindful around her baby, she was now actually

present for the experience. The implications of this for all our relationships are enormous. Imagine what it would be like to have
someone give you their full and undivided attention. Imagine what
it would be like to return the favour.

The monk with no time

So, the beauty of mindfulness is that you don't need to take extra
time out of your day to practise it. All it means is training your mind
to be present with the action, rather than being lost in thought
elsewhere. This answers those who argue that they have no time to
train the mind. A long time ago I heard about an American
meditation teacher who trained as a monk in Thailand. He'd gone
out there sometime back in the 1960s or 1970s, along with countless
others who were following the hippy trail across Asia at the time.
During his travels he became increasingly interested in meditation
and decided he wanted to study it full-time. Going to one of the most
renowned teachers in Thailand, he settled down in the monastery
and began his training, eventually becoming a monk. It was in many
ways a very strict training schedule and the day alternated between
periods of formal meditation and work. They would meditate for
something in the region of about eight hours a day.

If you haven't lived in a monastery, nunnery or retreat, then eight
hours probably sounds like quite a long time. But in the context of
these training centres, it's quite short. Of course, the rest of the time
was also spent training the mind, but in the form of mindfulness,
applying awareness to the chores of everyday life. Now because
there was a fairly well-established travelling route through Asia at
that time, a lot of other Westerners visited the monastery while he
was staying there. Many would stay a few weeks and then move on
in their travels. But while staying at the monastery they inevitably
fell into conversation with the Westerners who lived there. It was
during these conversations that this man heard how in the
monasteries of neighbouring Burma, residents were doing more like
eighteen hours a day of formal meditation. Being very enthusiastic
and wanting to move on quickly with his meditation, he started to

think seriously about moving. But he felt torn because the teacher he was studying with was so well known, so well respected.

A few months went by as he wrestled with the idea of leaving. If enlightenment was the game, then surely he'd stand more chance doing eighteen hours of meditation a day in one of the Burmese monasteries. Currently, he had so many different jobs to do – cleaning, collecting firewood, sewing monks' robes and so on – that he felt as if there was no time to meditate at all. Besides, he was finding the training difficult and suspected that the work was somehow interfering with his progress. After a while he went to see his teacher to tell him that he was going to leave. He was secretly hoping that his teacher would see how devoted and dedicated he was and give him the opportunity to stay and do the extra meditation where he was, but instead the teacher just calmly nodded his head at the news.

The man, by now somewhat incensed by his teacher's seemingly indifferent reaction, was at a loss. 'But don't you want to know *why* I'm leaving?' he asked. 'OK,' replied the teacher very calmly, still unmoved by his visitor. 'It's because we have no time to meditate here,' the man replied. 'Apparently in Burma they sit for eighteen hours a day, whereas here we do no more than eight hours a day. How can I make any progress if all I'm doing is cooking and cleaning and sewing all day? There's no time here!' I'm told the teacher looked at him earnestly, but with a smile on his face as he asked, 'Are you telling me you've no time to be mindful? Are you telling me that you have no time to be aware?' So caught up in his internal dialogue, at first the man missed the point altogether and shot back, 'Exactly. We're always so busy working that there's no time to be present.' The teacher laughed. 'So,' he replied, 'you're telling me that when you're sweeping the courtyard there's no time to be aware of the action of sweeping? That when you're pressing the monks' robes there's no time to be aware of the action of ironing? The point of training the mind is to become more aware. You have the same amount of time to do this whether you're sitting in the temple with your eyes closed or whether you're sweeping the courtyard with your eyes open!'

The man apparently fell quite silent, realising his misunderstanding of mind training. Like so many people, myself included, he'd thought that it was only possible to train the mind while sitting completely still in meditation. But mind training is so much more flexible than that. The practice of mindfulness shows us how we can apply the same quality of mind to everything we do. It doesn't matter whether we live a very physical life or a sedentary life, there is just as much time to be aware cycling down the road as there is sitting in a chair at home. And nor does it matter what type of job we have. We all follow the same twenty-four-hour clock, so we all have the same amount of time to train in awareness. Whether we're aware of the physical senses, our emotions, our thoughts, or the content of those thoughts, it's all awareness and there is always time to be aware.

The dot-to-dot day

Do you remember those dot-to-dot drawings from your early days at school? The ones that mapped out a picture with very small dots? In fact, they were so close together that all you needed to do was join the dots to feel as if you'd created some kind of masterpiece. This idea of dot-to-dot is a simple way of demonstrating how mindfulness can be so much more than just an isolated meditation exercise done once a day. Take a blank piece of paper and try drawing a straight line very slowly across the page. Even if you've got a very good eye, my guess is that there'll be at least a few wobbles along the way. If you haven't got a steady hand, the wobbles might be considerably greater. Let's say that this line symbolises your continuity of awareness throughout the day. When you're aware, you tend to have a sense of calm, of focus, of direction. And remember, even if you're not necessarily experiencing a pleasant emotion, you'll still have a sense of space around the emotions, some increased perspective, and some emotional stability. However, much like the line you drew across the page, for most people this idea of continuity of awareness tends to look very shaky.

Perhaps you wake up feeling great, thinking it's the weekend. But then you realise it's actually a weekday and plunge into depression. You get up, trip over the cat, swear out loud, and go to the bathroom. Eating breakfast, you cheer up a little and you start to think that it might not be such a bad day after all. Then you get an e-mail from your boss, just as you're leaving home, asking you to work late that day. 'Typical,' you think, 'it's always me.' Walking out of the front door, slamming it behind you, this time you swear under your breath. When you get to work and realise that it's not just you, but that everyone has been asked to work late, you somehow feel better. Then you notice the big plate of cakes on the table. You smile, as a wave of desire hits you. 'Must be someone's birthday,' you think to yourself, 'roll on coffee break.' But then you start thinking about the cakes a little more. You've been on a diet recently and have been doing so well, do you really want to eat the cake? Then again, you've also been working on being more kind to yourself, so perhaps you *should* eat the cake. You feel confused. You want the cake, you don't want the cake. And so the day goes on, forever caught up in the highs and lows of all that's going on around you. The one thing that remains the same throughout the day is that your thinking dictates the way you feel. In the absence of awareness, the realm of thought takes over.

Now try imagining it a different way. This time imagine that the piece of paper has lots of very small dots on it, going from one side to the other. Each dot is very close to the next one on the page. Now try drawing the same straight line. My guess is it's much easier now. All you have to do is focus on getting from one dot to the next. You don't have to think as far ahead as the other side of the piece of paper, but just a few millimetres to reach the next dot. All of a sudden it's not so difficult to draw a straight line. And if we continue the analogy of the line representing your sense of awareness (and therefore your emotional stability) throughout the day, then this is obviously very good news.

Rather than thinking of just being mindful during your ten

minutes of meditation each morning (and then trying to make it through the next twenty-three hours and fifty minutes of your day until you meditate again) maybe start to think of mindfulness in terms of something you can apply throughout your day. Remember, all it means is to give your full attention to whatever you're doing, whenever you're doing it. The implication of this is that it's simply no longer possible to think about where you'd rather be, what you'd rather be doing, or wishing that things were different from the way they are (all the types of thinking that usually leave you feeling stressed out), because you'll be present with whatever you're doing instead.

So, rather than plunging into a bad mood when you realise it's a weekday, instead you witness your response to that realisation and watch how the feeling comes and then goes. Having tripped over the cat, rather than swearing out loud and blaming it on your feline friend, you bend down to make sure it's OK, focusing on the wellbeing of the cat rather than your own internal frustrations. Forgetting your frustration in this simple act of altruism you start the day afresh. And so it goes on, moving from one activity to the next with purpose, focus and awareness.

The distracted man

This idea of being aware and awake to each and every new moment is potentially very exciting. It's so easy to live life on autopilot and for the days and years to pass us by. A client came to see me at the clinic some time back. He came not because he had been referred by his GP, or because he was suffering from some kind of mental illness – he came because he said he was feeling increasingly disconnected from the world around him, increasingly caught up in thoughts about work, and he didn't know what to do about it. Not only was this affecting the way he felt within himself, but it was also starting to affect his relationships. He said his wife was fed up with him never listening to what she was saying (which he confirmed as being true), and that his children were always complaining that he was never there. In fact, one of them had recently told him that even when he *was* there, it was as though he was off somewhere else in his head. This comment had been the final straw. He felt heartbroken to hear that from one of his own children. Understandably, he was very upset and he worried that if he didn't do something to change the situation, then the ramifications for the family unit would be very serious.

For the first couple of weeks we worked together to establish a really strong foundation for mindfulness, in particular the meditation element, taking ten minutes out of each day to allow the mind to settle. At first he struggled with this idea. 'I'm already finding it difficult to find time for my family, how can I justify taking out even *more* time for myself? Isn't that just selfish?' This is a common viewpoint, but if you think about it, that's not really the way it is. So I explained, 'What you're doing here is training your mind so that you can actually be there for others. How can you be happy and feel connected with others if you are always caught up in your own thoughts? So, far from taking something away from your family, you're actually giving them something. You're giving them a better husband, a better father, someone who is truly there for them.' It took no more than a week or so for him to experience that connection in a very direct and tangible way. In fact, he returned with a big smile on his face the following session and proudly exclaimed, 'I haven't shouted at the kids all week!'

By the time we came to the third week, I was keen to introduce him to walking meditation. Not the formal kind which is usually done very, very slowly, but more in the way of being mindful when out and about, walking at an ordinary speed. This is usually the point when the 'mindfulness penny' drops, when it starts to make sense that training the mind is about so much more than sitting down with your eyes closed. Having walked together around the block a few times as I explained the technique, I then sent him off to do a short exercise on his own. The first part of the exercise was on very quiet streets, where it was easier to concentrate. The second part was along a very busy road with lots of cars and pedestrians. Ten minutes later he returned to the clinic from his walk.

'I've lived just round the corner from here for fifteen years,' he said, 'and I walk down this same street nearly every single day. But that's the first time, the very first time, I've ever actually *seen* the street. I know that sounds ridiculous, but it's true. It's the first time I've noticed the colour of the houses, the cars in the driveways, the smell of the flowers, the sounds of the birds.' But it's what he said next that really struck me. With a genuine sense of remorse he said, 'Where have I *been* all my life?'

How many of us live our lives in this way? Swept away by memories of the past and plans for the future. So preoccupied with thinking that we're completely unaware of what's actually taking place right now, oblivious to life unfolding around us. The present moment just feels so ordinary that we take it for granted, and yet that's what makes it so *extraordinary* – the fact that we so rarely experience the present moment exactly as it is. And quite unlike anything else in life, you don't need to go anywhere to get it, or do anything to create it. It's right here, no matter what you're doing. It's in the eating of a sandwich, the drinking of a cup of tea, the washing of the dishes . . . ordinary, everyday activities. This is what it means to be mindful, to be present, to be aware.

The juggling monk

When I was a monk there were a lot of things that I wasn't allowed to do. Well, yes, obviously there was that one, but there were other things too. Now this is fine when you live in a monastery, because the day is structured in such a way that you are pretty much always engaged with either meditation or work of some kind. So it's not as though you're sitting there thinking what you'd do if you were not a monk. Besides, everyone around you is doing the same thing, so there's not so much to compare your life to. But when you live as a monk outside of the monastery you lose that structure, and life becomes a little more complicated. In fact, it becomes that much more important to engage with activities that are, how can I put it . . . equally wholesome. Now my apartment in Moscow was very old, built way back in the days of the Soviet Empire. In my first winter, before I'd learnt the art of double glazing with newspaper and cellophane wrap, the ice was thick on the inside of the windows. The wallpaper hung desperately to the wall in just a few places and random bits of metal poked out of the concrete ceiling. But the location more than made up for it. It was right on the edge of a large lake in the north-west of the city, famous for its clean air and sandy beaches.

It obviously wasn't appropriate to sunbathe as a monk, but during the hot summer months I often used to go down to the park next to the lake and juggle. 'You did what?' I hear you say. 'You mean that it wasn't appropriate to sunbathe but that it was OK to juggle like Coco the Clown?' Well, yes and no. It was certainly appropriate to find an enjoyable way to relax outside of the formal meditation practice, and for me this meant juggling. I guess I could have sat in my flat and meditated all day, every day, but the need to move and be physical once in a while was surprisingly strong. So I would juggle, often for many hours at a time. I found that the act of juggling perfectly mirrored my meditation. It became an external reflection of what was happening inside. If my mind was too tight, too focused, then the juggling balls didn't flow. On the other hand, if the mind was too loose and I wasn't concentrating enough, then I would drop the balls altogether. So there was something in working with this balance of focus and relaxation, which reflected the inner balance developed through meditation. I guess it's what most people would describe as being 'in the zone' and you've no doubt experienced it yourself at some time, perhaps while you were playing a sport, painting a picture, cooking a meal, or doing some other form of activity.

One day I was juggling five balls. If you've ever juggled, you'll know that each extra ball you add takes that little bit longer to master. For example, if you learnt to juggle three balls in a week, then it might take a whole month to learn how to juggle four, and then perhaps six months to learn how to juggle five. I was a good few months into learning five balls at the time and, on the whole, was able to keep them all in the air at any one time. But it wasn't pretty. I was still rushing in my mind, frantically trying to correct and over-correct the rise and the fall of each ball. It really does take a genuine sense of relaxation and ease for the balls to flow evenly and smoothly. Then one time I forgot to try. Strange as that may sound, I just forgot. I was thinking about something else momentarily before I started to juggle and so there was none of the usual effort, anticipation and expectation of what was to come. I just threw the balls up and started to juggle. The result was something quite extraordinary. In fact, it wouldn't have looked at all out of place in the *Matrix*. It was a total distortion of time as I knew it. Sure, I'd had meditation sessions where fifty minutes had felt like five minutes and, more frequently, sessions where five minutes had felt like fifty minutes, but never had I seen this quite so clearly while engaged in an everyday activity (if you can call juggling an everyday activity). In that moment I had all the time in the world. It was as if the balls just hung there in the air. I had time to look at them, each and every one, thinking how I would move this one over to the left a little bit and that one slightly to the right. It was as if someone had pressed a slow motion button, an extraordinary thing. When I quit rushing around in my mind, trying to get from one ball to the next, trying to control every little thing, there was an inexplicable amount of time and space. It might be something to think about given the way we rush around in life. It doesn't mean you can't do things quickly and still be mindful – of course you can. It just means that the body moving quickly and the mind being in a rush are two very different things.

The patient yogi

It seems fitting to finish this section with a story I heard from one of my teachers while training as a monk. At first glance it may not seem to have anything to do with everyday life, but actually says a great deal about the spirit of mindfulness, how it can be used and also how easily the essence of it can be missed. The story involves a yogi in Tibet who was doing a special type of meditation technique based on developing patience. An impatient yogi? Really? Well, yes, impatience is universal. It doesn't matter whether you're a mum or dad at home struggling with the sleepless nights of a newborn, a commuter waiting for your train, or a yogi sitting on top of a mountain relentlessly pursuing enlightenment, everyone experiences impatience at one time or another.

Having become increasingly aware of his impatience, the yogi had gone to his teacher and been given the instructions for this particular meditation technique. He'd then gone off into the mountains to find a cave to live in while he practised it. If you're wondering how he would survive all alone in the mountains, they actually have a wonderful system of support there, whereby local villagers transport basic food supplies up the mountain every now and then. This way, the yogi, or yogini as the female counterpart is known, can be far enough away from potential distractions but close enough to be assisted by others. Anyway, this yogi had found himself a nice cave and soon got down to the task of discovering his inherent patience which his teacher had assured him was there. Several months went by and still the yogi continued to meditate. The people in the local village were really impressed.

Not long after, a visiting teacher came to the village. He was a very well-known man whom the locals had a lot of respect for and they were keen to tell him about 'one of their own' who was diligently practising in a mountain cave. The teacher became intrigued and asked if he could visit the yogi. At first the locals said it would be impossible, that he was in a strict, cloistered retreat. But as this teacher was so insistent, and so well respected, they eventually pointed him in the direction of the cave. When the teacher finally reached the cave and had regained his breath, he peered into the darkness to look for the yogi. Seeing him sitting there in meditation, he coughed a little, just to make the yogi aware that he was present. The yogi didn't move. So the teacher coughed a little louder. This time the yogi opened one eye to see who it was and, not recognising the teacher, closed it again without saying a word. The teacher wasn't sure what to do. He didn't want to disturb the yogi, but at the same time he was keen to find out more about this practice of patience the yogi had been given.

So the next time the teacher coughed even louder and said, 'Excuse me, sorry to bother you, but could I have just a moment of your time please?' The yogi said nothing, but seemed to look a little unsettled by the intrusion. The teacher repeated his request. This time the yogi's eyes opened wide and he finally spoke. 'Can you not see that I'm trying to meditate here? I have a very important practice on patience which I'm trying to complete.' 'I know,' said the teacher, 'that's what I wanted to talk to you about.' The yogi inhaled sharply and then let out a big sigh. 'Please, just leave me alone, I don't want to talk to you.' The yogi closed his eyes and went back to his meditation. Undeterred, the teacher continued in his efforts to speak to the yogi. 'But that's what I wanted to talk to you about,' he said. 'I hear you've really made a lot of progress with this practice and I'm keen to hear about your experience.' By now the yogi was ready to let rip. He'd come all the way up into the mountains to get away from distractions and yet here he was having to deal with this man. So in no uncertain terms he told the teacher where to go, only part of which involved going down the mountain.

The teacher remained outside the cave for a few minutes more before deciding to give it one last try. Calling out to the yogi, he said, 'Tell me, what have you learnt about patience from your meditation?' The yogi, unable to contain himself for a moment longer, jumped up from his seat, grabbed some loose stones off the floor and started to hurl them at the man in the cave entrance. By now he was screaming at the top of his voice, 'How can I meditate on patience when you constantly interrupt me the whole time?' Incensed, he chased the man away by continuing to throw stones at him. When the yogi had finally run out of stones, the teacher looked back to make one final comment. 'So,' he said with a big smile on his face, 'I see the meditation on patience is going well.'

Meditation is undoubtedly a vital cornerstone to the practice of mindfulness. To practise mindfulness in everyday life without doing even ten minutes of meditation a day is a bit like trying to build the foundations of a house on loose gravel. It will work, but it will not be anywhere near as stable as if you built it on solid ground. However, the reverse is also true. What good is meditation if it doesn't change the way you feel and behave in life? Remember, the point of getting more headspace is to make your own life and the lives of the people around you more comfortable. It's not much good getting all nice and calm if you plan to lose it with the very first person you come into contact with. Try to think about meditation as the platform from which you'll operate over the next twenty-four hours. That sense of calm will enable you to respond skilfully to situations if you can maintain your awareness. But if you get so caught up with your own story, that you lose all awareness, then you may well find that you react just as impulsively as the yogi.

Mindfulness exercises for everyday life

While it's a wonderful feeling to sit down for ten minutes or more each day to practise a meditation technique, the concept of mindfulness really comes into its own when you start to apply it to everyday life. In this part of the book I've put together a few of my favourite mindfulness exercises for everyday living. They include mindfulness for eating, walking, exercising and sleeping. As before, although it might be tempting to jump straight to the technique at the end of each section, there is much more to these exercises than a simple list of instructions. The introduction and story for each activity will hopefully convey the flavour of the technique, while demonstrating its full potential.

Headspace for eating

How often do you actually *taste* the food you eat? Most people tend to acknowledge the first few bites, just to ensure they're eating what they think they're supposed to be, and then slip into a semi-conscious state of eating. I don't mean some kind of semi-*comatose* state, but rather involvement in other activities, such as thinking. As it's not particularly complicated to move a fork back and forwards from a plate, or a sandwich from hand to mouth, we've developed an ability to carry out the task without even thinking about it, in much the same way we have with walking.

For fans of multitasking this probably sounds like a dream come true. It means we can sit and eat our food while reading the newspaper, working on the computer, speaking on the phone, or mentally working through our plans for the evening or weekend ahead. It's equally common in the evenings, when we get home late from work feeling tired, already thinking about having to get up early the next morning or perhaps putting the kids to bed. The result is a meal prepared in the shortest possible time, cooked in the shortest possible time, and then eaten in the shortest possible time. This assumes we haven't just grabbed some fast-food on the way home from work and finished it before we've even walked in the front door. I'm not saying this is wrong, this book isn't written to tell you *what* you should eat, *where* you should eat it and *how* you should do it. That's up to you. But I would like to briefly explain how mindfulness and meditation can be applied to the simple act of eating with some remarkable benefits.

The five-star monastery

In contrast to the hurried mealtimes that most of us experience, mealtimes at the monastery were generally a sedate and dignified affair, with a few notable exceptions I might add. When you don't have much else to focus on, food takes on an extraordinary importance, as do the other simple things in life such as having a cup of tea, or taking a warm shower. These things are described as 'sensory pleasures' in the monastic tradition and, as a general rule, we were encouraged not to indulge in them too much. They were seen as additional activities to train in mindfulness rather than luxuries to indulge in. However, I trust it now goes without saying that this way of living is very specific to the monastery and you shouldn't feel for one moment as though you need to deny yourself the simple pleasures in life to get the full benefit from your meditation.

There was one Western monastery where I lived (the one with high walls again) that had its own unique approach to food, as it did to everything else. When I arrived on my first day I was asked to make a list of all my favourite foods and drinks. 'Wow,' I thought, 'this is amazing. It's like a five-star monastery.' I was also asked to make a list of all the foods and drinks I didn't like. Again, I thought, 'Wow, this is so considerate.' They even had three meals a day, eating dinner in the evening. It felt like moving into the Four Seasons of Buddhist monasteries. So, you can probably imagine my disappoint-ment when dinner was served up with many of the things I'd put on the list as not liking. In fact, as I looked more closely at the plate, it appeared as though pretty much everything had come from that list. Had there been some kind of mix-up, some kind of mistake? Perhaps I'd got the two pieces of paper mixed up.

It turns out that there'd not been any mistake at all. In fact, the reason for asking those questions had been merely to ensure that we were not indulging in foods that we enjoyed. It was also to ensure that we had, and I quote, 'the opportunity to examine the experience of dislike'. As if the food wasn't bad enough, I was then given coffee afterwards. Now in my experience coffee is pretty much a love or hate affair for most people and I really disliked it. Sure, it smelt great, but the taste was horrible and I disliked the jittery sensations it left me with afterwards. And yet here were these monks serving me up a mugful just a couple of hours before going to bed. In addition to feeling nauseous while drinking it, I was absolutely wired all night. And, as I soon found out, this was something to be repeated on a regular basis during my stay there. I guess my reasons for scaling the wall after a few months are becoming more obvious. But there was a funny side to this too. Conscious of the fact that I didn't want to turn into a whale, eating three meals a day while doing nothing but sitting on my backside meditating, I had written down things like chocolate, biscuits and cake on the 'I don't like . . .' list, thinking that it was an easy way of making sure I ate a healthy diet. Little had I known that this was to be my 'He must eat . . .' list, and I was therefore served up chocolate and cake at the end of every evening meal, much to the annoyance of the other monks.

While this approach may sound extreme, until then I'd never really thought about why I liked and disliked certain foods. I had always assumed I 'just did'. Having the opportunity to become more aware of the process was definitely beneficial and, to my surprise, I actually started to eat many of the foods that I'd never liked. Once I'd got over the initial resistance and all the mental chatter around it, I found that the direct *experience* of the food was quite different to my *idea* of it. Similarly, foods that I'd once enjoyed as an idea, but were probably not all that good for me, became less of an obsession. Once the desire had faded away somewhat and I actually started paying close attention to how the food made me feel, suddenly it didn't look quite so appetising, at least not in the quantities that I might have previously consumed.

It's perhaps no surprise then that 'mindful eating' is being touted as the next wonder diet. There's no question that mindfulness can fundamentally change your relationship to food (including your food choices, the quantity you eat, and the way in which you eat it), but it doesn't really do mindfulness justice to think of it purely in terms of the next weight-loss sensation. The reason I say this is because there can then be a danger of confusing *mindfulness* as a way to happiness with *weight-loss* as a way to happiness. They are two very different things, the latter offering no lasting sense of fulfilment or headspace whatsoever. However, developing a healthy relationship with food can only be a good thing and, if you can lose some excess weight as a result of being more mindful around food, then that's a wonderful thing. It comes back to that same idea of having greater perspective, the necessary space in which to respond skilfully rather than acting impulsively.

I've met very few people who are completely comfortable around food, who have no hang-ups about what they eat. Most people I speak to say that they often feel guilty about their eating habits, that there is always this gap between what they 'want' to eat and what they think they 'should' eat. This definitely used to be the case for me. Before I went away to train as a monk I was fanatical about food. I was competing in gymnastics at the time and training in the gym every day, completely obsessed with fitness. I would plan my meals for the week down to the last ounce, weighing out just the right amount of food for each meal. I avoided anything that would be considered even remotely enjoyable by most people's standards, even when I went out for a meal. If a craving for anything sweet came along I'd just push it back down to wherever it came from. I became so fanatical about it that I would even phone ahead to the restaurant I was going out to and order something special in advance (egg white omelette anyone?). There was very little mindfulness in this way of living. It was an extreme, and extremes are rarely a healthy way of living, no matter which end of the scale they may be. So when I went away to the monastery I had a lot to learn about just how much emotional attachment I had to my eating habits. There are many stories to choose from to illustrate this, but the one that highlights the emotional relationship we have with food is what has become known as 'the ice-cream story'.

The ice-cream story

Mealtimes in the Burmese monastery were solemn affairs. In fairness, it was a silent monastery so there wasn't really that much to communicate anyway. And besides, mealtimes were designed to be formal eating meditation sessions. We'd sit on the floor around big circular tables, with about six monks to each table. It was a big monastery, with well over eighty monks, so the dining room was quite big. There were nuns too, but they remained hidden on the other side of the dining room separated from us by large and seemingly insurmountable wooden screens. The rest of the room was quite open, which meant that we looked out on the monastery gardens. It was a very pleasant place to be.

It didn't matter whether it was breakfast or lunch, the food was always the same, curry and rice. The curry was thick and oily (not great for digestion), but always tasted good. A bowl and a spoon would be sitting waiting on the table when we arrived, and two monks would then come around and dish out the rice and curry. Following a short verse or two of traditional text, a gong would be sounded and we'd have an hour to eat the food. When I say an hour, I mean an hour – no more, and no less. At this particular monastery everything was done very, very, *very* slowly. I mean it might take twenty seconds even to get the rice from the plate to your mouth, never mind eating it. There was a good reason for this of course as it allowed us to examine the workings of the mind in a very detailed way. But it was slow, very, very slow. By breakfast time I was often really hungry and would just dive into the food without really thinking much about it. I would then feel a hand on my shoulder. It was the hand of the discipline master whose job it was to make sure that everyone was conducting themselves in a manner both conducive to training and befitting a monk. I got to know the discipline master very well during my stay there.

There are certain days of the year in Burma when members of the local community are given time off from their jobs to come and practise meditation at the monastery. I'm not sure if they were very enthusiastic meditators or were just happy to have the day off work, but lots of people would visit on these days. When they came they would often bring food to donate to the monastery kitchen. It might be sacks of rice, vegetables, or even meat and fish. One day a man arrived with several big shiny containers, almost like oil drums. I had no idea what was inside, but it was unusual for a lay-person to come into the dining room during a mealtime. There was something else different that day too. The bowls and spoons that were usually on the table waiting for us were not there. I could see the two monks who usually handed out the food making their way towards our side of the dining room, but rather than carrying the usual pans of rice and curry, they were handing out very small dishes with something yellow inside. Almost like busy waiters in a restaurant, they were hurriedly moving backwards and forwards from the kitchen handing out these small bowls. And from what I could see through the small gaps in the screen down the middle of the room, the same thing was happening on the other side of the room.

I suddenly realised what it was. The monks were handing out ice-cream! Now before I get too carried away, just momentarily pause and consider what it would be like to eat the same curry and rice every day and never to have anything different. OK, so now imagine someone serves you up a bowl of ice-cream. Pretty exciting, right? Well, I was excited – however ridiculous it sounds, I genuinely felt a rush of excitement. It was like being a child at a birthday party when the cake comes out. One by one the bowls were handed out to every monk and nun. I stared at the ice-cream. It was summertime, over 40 degrees . . . the clock was ticking. But of course nobody could begin until the gong had been struck. I grew quickly impatient, my concern for the ice-cream's longevity far exceeding that which is appropriate for any human being to feel towards a frozen ball of cream and sugar. Of course, there was nothing wrong or even unusual in my reaction, but it would be fair to say that my levels of desire and craving at this point were nearing the far end of the scale.

Then I saw what the hold-up was. The two monks who'd placed the ice-cream in front of us were now going around putting our regular bowls and spoons down on the table. I started to talk to myself. 'It's OK, the bowls are empty, this won't take long, the ice-cream will last.' But by the time they finally reached our table I could see that what they were doing was pushing the bowls of ice-cream towards the middle of the table and placing the empty bowl and spoon in front of it. Behind them, two other monks were walking around with the pans of rice and curry, filling the bowls up. It was then that I realised what was happening: we would have to eat the curry before the ice-cream. Now in the privacy of my own home and with no speed restrictions I would have fancied my chances, but not here, not in the monastery. It would take almost an hour to eat the curry and rice and I was quite certain the discipline master would make sure of it.

I felt a surge of anger, closely followed by lots of angry-looking thoughts. 'This is ridiculous! It's torture! What a waste of food! I thought Buddhism was supposed to be about kindness, there's nothing kind about this! And what about that lovely man who'd spent his money on this ice-cream, had they given a moment's thought to how he might feel?' Some of the thoughts went further still as I mechanically moved the fork in slow motion back and forth from the plate, looking longingly at the melting ball of ice-cream. I had no headspace and no sense of awareness. Far from being mindful, I was entirely absorbed in my own thoughts. In fact, I was so absorbed in my own thoughts that I couldn't even see that in reality the real cause of anger was simply me not getting what I wanted. I guess you could call it attachment, wanting something so much that when you don't get it you resist, you struggle. Well, I was struggling all right, no doubt about it.

Funnily enough, people often get angry on my behalf when I tell them this story. But remember, I was staying at the monastery of my own free will and could get up and leave at any time. I was a willing participant in these situations and felt that I had something to learn from the experiences. It's just that sometimes I got so caught up in my own thoughts and feelings that I temporarily forgot to be aware of this simple fact. Once again, this approach is specific to monastic training, you don't need to torture yourself with melting ice-cream to get the most from your meditation. There will be plenty of other situations that will come along quite naturally in life that will test the stability of your own awareness and compassion.

After a while of thinking and feeling this way the momentum of anger started to fade, and was replaced by a wave of sadness and guilt. I felt sad about indulging in all those angry thoughts, and guilty about where and to whom they'd been directed. This feeling remained for a while longer, again accompanied by thoughts that reflected this passing mood. Finally, the ball of ice-cream lost its battle with the midday sun and all that was left in the bowl was a pool of warm, yellow, sticky goo. As I looked at it, I found it hard to imagine why I'd got quite so upset about it. Or why I'd got quite so excited about it. It didn't look nearly as appetising now. And with those thoughts came a wave of acceptance that seemed to transform my mood altogether. My emotional attachment to the ice-cream (the fact it happened to be food was incidental) had been so strong that I'd lost all sense of awareness. And this loss of awareness had resulted not only in endless, exhausting and ultimately futile mental chatter, but had also left me with the feeling of having been swept away on an emotional roller-coaster from which there was no getting off.

This may be an extreme example, but it highlights a common experience with food. It's the sense that we're so absorbed in our feelings, or in the constant mental chatter, that we no longer feel in control of our choices and actions. Have you ever found yourself halfway through a chocolate bar or a packet of crisps, only to think, 'Why am I even eating this?' Oblivious to the fact that we might not even be hungry, we mindlessly follow every impulse that arises. This isn't helped by the fact that we're so often distracted by other things at the same time. In fact, it just makes it all the more likely that we'll remain lost in the world of thought. I know it sounds old-fashioned, but when did you last sit at the table to eat a meal? For most people, the sofa has taken the place of the table. In the past we'd have paused before food, whether that was down to etiquette or prayer. It was a time to acknowledge what was about to be eaten, to get a sense of appreciation for having food in front of us.

With this in mind, I'm going to suggest that this following exercise is done while sitting at a table. You may like to try it alone the first couple of times, as you'll probably find it easier to concentrate. It's best done in silence to begin with, free from conversation or background noise, so you'll find it easier if you turn off the television, any music, and yes, even your mobile phone. You'll also get more out of it if you do it without any reading material in front of you, so say goodbye to your laptop, books and magazines. This leaves just you and your food. People often say they feel either lonely or bored when they first try this exercise (an indication of just how rarely we're undistracted in this way), but as soon as you throw yourself into the exercise, both of these feelings will fade quite quickly. You may also like to eat a little more slowly during this exercise (although not as slowly as in the Burmese monastery) so that it's easier to apply the instructions. This is not the way (or the speed) I'm suggesting you eat *all* the time, but as a formal exercise it's best done this way. It's the difference between meditation and mindfulness that we discussed before. Meditation simply helps you be more mindful in everyday life, no matter how busy you are, or how many people you're with. So once you're familiar with what it means to eat mindfully, you can apply it to all your mealtimes, even if you're chatting among friends or eating in a hurry.

Exercise 7: eating meditation

This exercise is also available as a guided meditation at www.get someheadspace.com/headspace-book/get-some-headspace

Sit down at a table, preferably alone, and free from any external distractions. Don't worry too much if there are external sounds that are out of your control as you can build these into the exercise, in just the same way as you did with Take10.
Before you pick up the food to eat, take a couple of deep breaths – in through the nose and out through the mouth – to allow the body and mind to settle a little.

Next, take a moment to appreciate the food. Where has

it come from? What country? Was it grown or was it manufactured? Try and imagine the different ingredients in their natural growing environment and even the types of people who would have been looking after the crops or animals. Over time we've become completely disconnected from the origins of the food in our diet. That may not sound particularly important, but in terms of having a broader sense of mindfulness around food, then it can be really very helpful.

As you do this, notice if there is any sense of impatience in the mind, of just wanting to get on and eat the food. Perhaps you're thinking of all the things that you need to 'get on and do'. Whatever the reaction, it's most likely just conditioned behaviour, a habit, but one that you may well find surprisingly strong.

Now without going on some kind of guilt trip, take a moment to appreciate the fact that you actually have food on your plate. We can sometimes forget that for many people in the world this will not be the case at all. This may not be something you like to think about, but there's something really valuable in this process, a sense of appreciation and gratitude is at the heart of a stable mindfulness practice.

As I say, this next part you may want to do a little more slowly than usual, but no matter how you do it, do it naturally and without thinking too much about it.

If it's a food you're going to eat with the hands, then notice the texture as you pick it up, the temperature, and perhaps the colour(s). If it's from a plate, then notice instead the texture and temperature of the cutlery as you move it towards the food, but taking the time to notice the colours on the plate.

As you move the food towards your mouth, shift the focus away from the hands and more towards the eyes, nose and mouth. How does it smell? What does it look like up close? And, as you put it in your mouth, what is the taste, the texture, the temperature? You don't need to 'do' anything. You're simply observing the different bodily senses at work.

In addition to the physical senses, notice how the mind

responds to the food. For example, is the food met with pleasure or displeasure in your mind? Is there acceptance of the food as it is, or maybe some resistance to certain aspects of it? Perhaps it's too hot, too cold, too sweet, or too sour. Notice how the mind rushes to judge the food and to make comparisons with previous meals.

Once you've taken a few mouthfuls you may find that the mind starts to get bored with the exercise and will wander off into thinking about something else. As with Take10, this is normal and nothing to worry about. In the same way as before, as soon as you realise it's wandered off, just gently bring your attention back to the object of meditation – the process of eating and the different tastes, smells, textures, sights and even sounds involved.

As you continue your meal in this way you can start to notice whether there's a strong habitual urge to eat more quickly, perhaps to move closer to dessert! Or maybe there are feelings of unease about what you're eating, especially if you are body-conscious. Notice as these different thoughts arise in the mind and, if you can, also notice how the breath appears as you eat. The breath may well give you some indication of how comfortable or uncomfortable this exercise is for you.

As you move towards the end of the meal, notice if perhaps there's a sense of disappointment at having nearly finished, or relief in having nearly finished. Maybe even take a little extra time to savour the final mouthful.

Before getting up to leave or moving on to the next thing to eat, take a couple of deep breaths again. Remind yourself of how the plate looked when it was full of food and how it looks now, empty with nothing on it. Notice how, in contrast, before you sat down the stomach felt empty and how now it feels full. By noticing these things, noticing how everything is always changing, how everything has both a beginning and an end, the mind tends to experience a greater sense of ease over time.

Headspace for walking

Have you ever started walking down a street, only to find yourself a few minutes later at the end of the street, but not really sure how you got there? This is a common experience and one that raises the question, if you were not present 'in the street', where were you? Almost inevitably you will have been caught up in the thoughts of the mind. Of course sometimes it's nice to just let the mind wander and many people say this is when they are at their most creative. Only you truly know how much of the mental chatter is productive or pleasant when you're out and about. Now walking down the street, the implications of drifting off into thought are usually not all that serious. But have you ever done the same with driving? Suddenly realised that you've driven a couple of miles down a familiar route with no sense of awareness whatsoever? It's both funny and scary. Funny that we could ever be so absent minded, and scary because of the implications. But there's a very good reason why this sort of thing happens to us, and it's more obvious than you might think.

Walking is an established and habituated action that requires very little concentration. Because of this, it's almost become autonomous, and it's easy to slip into a semi-conscious state of walking, where the legs are moving but the mind is thinking about something different altogether. It might be thinking about things that are already on your mind (this includes all the little things as well as the big stuff), or it might be that new thoughts are triggered by external objects or other people in the street. This is especially true if you live in a busy city or a very crowded place with lots of activity.

Noticing these things is fine. In fact, from a mindfulness perspective you could even say it's good, because it means you are, temporarily outside of the realm of thought. The problem arises once you engage with the thing that's grabbed your attention and when you then start to think about it, to create a story around it. Perhaps when a noisy car goes past it reminds you that you don't like living in a busy place and you start dreaming of where you might like to live instead. Or maybe when you see something in the shop window you start to think how nice it would be to have it, only to then start thinking about your money troubles. Whatever it is that causes the mind to wander off, it's a movement *away* from the present moment, away from the direct experience of life. It can sometimes feel as though we're so busy remembering, planning and analysing life, that we forget to *experience* life – as it *actually* is, rather than how we think it *should be*.

As with most of these exercises, there are two ways to approach training the mind to be present while walking. First there's the formal approach, which I'll refer to as 'walking meditation', which tends to be done a little more slowly. And then there's the more general, practical application of mindfulness for walking in everyday life. It's not necessary to do both and many people jump straight into the general application because it doesn't require any more time out of the day. You probably already walk a lot throughout the day anyway, so all you're doing is directing the mind in a different way as you continue to do what you've always done. The way I've structured the next exercise is a fusion of these two approaches. I would suggest, if you have time, that you try it more slowly at first, if only once or twice, just to get a better feel for the technique. It might also be worth trying it in a park or on a quiet street rather than in the middle of a busy town. It's perhaps the equivalent of learning to swim in a swimming pool rather than the sea.

The zombies

During a stay in Australia I was lucky enough to spend some time working in a retreat in the Blue Mountains. The retreat house was set among the most beautiful countryside, just on the edge of a small, but fairly well-populated village. It was used by all sorts of different people, monks, nuns and lay-people alike. What with Australia not being a 'Buddhist' country, it was funded largely by donations from the local Sri Lankan and Burmese community. They would even bring the most incredible freshly cooked food for everyone to eat during the retreats. As one man who was staying there on retreat remarked, when asked how he was finding it all, 'Well, the bits *in-between* mealtimes are quite difficult, but the rest of the retreat is fantastic!' Being in the tradition of the Burmese monasteries, there was a strong emphasis placed on this formal style of walking meditation. People were usually given lessons on how to do it inside the retreat house, but because the grounds were so big and so beautiful people would often go outside to do it.

Now you probably need to see it to get a real sense of what this might look like, but let's just say that the scene wouldn't have looked out of place in a mental asylum. Wherever I looked there were people pacing backwards and forwards, very, very slowly, as they applied the instructions they'd been given. This scene was exaggerated by the fact that they'd been taught to look directly ahead, not making any eye contact with anyone else and certainly not talking.

A lot of visitors really enjoyed this exercise, as it meant they were not in the meditation hall, as they tried to last another hour with their legs tangled up in the lotus position. It also meant that they could be outside, enjoying the sunshine. But for many people it was the simple fact that walking meditation seemed to provide a much greater sense of ease and spaciousness than the sitting practice. And there's a good reason for this. When most people start to meditate they usually find it quite hard to get the amount of effort right. Try too hard and the meditation feels uncomfortable, but don't try enough and you fall asleep. It's that balance of focus and relaxation that I mentioned before. As a general rule, however, walking meditation seems to more naturally lend itself to the spacious element, so for many people this feels a lot more comfortable in the early days. I should add that walking meditation should not be considered a *replacement* for the seated meditation. Both have their place, but the sitting practice has its own particular importance.

All of the retreat participants were given strict instructions to only practise this walking technique *inside* the grounds of the retreat. But then as humans we're not always so good at following instructions and, sure enough, come lunchtime three or four of the students decided that it was time to expand their horizons and journey beyond the gate. Now just imagine you live in a lovely sleepy little village in the mountains, where you know all your neighbours and everyone knows you. And then one day you're staring out of the window, admiring the view, when you notice a man on the opposite side of the road, seemingly walking in slow motion, dressed in casual clothes, eyes fixed forward, oblivious to you standing in the window. Then you spot another one, this time a woman. She's not far behind the first man, in fact it looks as though they could almost be competing to see who can walk the slowest. And then you see another one, and another one. You don't recognise any of these people, and yet each one looks the same, as if they are in some kind of trance, zombies who don't have the strength to hold out their arms in front of them.

Now if you were to see this, you'd be entitled to be a little concerned. In fact, if you were of an anxious disposition, you may well lose it altogether. So it was no surprise when a local resident spotted this very same scene one day, and decided that the best course of action was to call the police. She figured that there must be some kind of brainwashing technique going on in the retreat and that people were just wandering out into the street in a semi-comatose state. The local police now have arguably the best understanding of walking meditation of any police department in the country.

This brings me to an important point. Walking meditation, even when done as a formal, structured practice, should not be done in some kind of robotic way. It simply requires you to walk *naturally*, but at a slightly slower pace. And if you're in a monastery or a retreat, then that pace might be very, very slow. But it's still a *natural* movement that doesn't require a lot of thinking. You know how to walk, you don't need to think about it. But for some reason (in just the way some people will inevitably 'over-think' the breath while doing their sitting meditation), some people will feel the urge to *think* about the process, rather than simply be aware of it. And this is when you can start to look rather strange. So don't try and walk in any special kind of way – it's just walking. The fact that you'll probably be doing this at your usual walking speed and possibly while talking to another person will hopefully dictate that you maintain a natural style. And that's part of the reason I'd encourage you to focus your efforts on mindfulness of walking in everyday life as soon as you are familiar with the exercise below.

When people come to the clinic, no matter whether they come for high blood pressure, insomnia, addiction, depression or anything else for that matter, they all learn how to apply the qualities of meditation and the principles of mindfulness to the act of walking. If you're going to make meditation work for you throughout the day I can't emphasise enough just how important this is. When people first try this technique they nearly all comment on how surreal it feels. A common phrase is 'I felt as though I was *in* life, but not *part* of it'. At the same time, acknowledging the paradox, they say they felt less separate from the world around them, a greater awareness of being interconnected in the world. Others comment on how vivid everything appears, how 'alive' the technique makes them feel. If we step out of thoughts for long enough to notice and appreciate the richness of life around us, then undoubtedly that's going to feel quite vivid compared to our usual dull state when we are lost in thought.

Exercise 8: walking meditation

This exercise is also available as a guided meditation at www.getsomeheadspace.com/headspace-book/get-some-headspace

As you begin to walk, notice how the body feels. Does it feel heavy or light, stiff or relaxed? Don't rush to answer the question, but take a few seconds to become aware of your posture and the way you're carrying yourself.

Without trying to change the way you're walking, simply observe how it feels. Much like the breath, the walking process is so automated and conditioned that you won't even need to think about it. So just take a moment to observe it, to notice it. It's quite common to feel self-conscious when you do this, but the feeling usually passes quite quickly.

While you won't need to think about the process of walking, you will need to be aware of what's going on around you, so take care to notice cars, other people, road signals and the like as you're doing the exercise.

Begin by noticing what you see going on around you. It might be people walking past, shop window displays, cars, advertisements and all the other things you'd expect to see around you in a busy city. If you live in the countryside, it's more likely to be fields, trees and animals instead. Notice the colours and shapes, the movement and perhaps the stillness too. There's no need to actually think about what you're seeing – simply to see it and acknowledge it is enough. Take about thirty seconds to do this.

Then turn your attention to sounds – what can you hear? Perhaps it's the sound of your feet on the pavement, of cars passing by, of birds in the trees or of people talking. Without getting caught up in thinking about the objects of sound, just take a moment to be aware of them, as though they are just coming and going in your field of awareness. Again, take about thirty seconds to do this.

Next turn your attention to smells for thirty seconds or so, some of which may be pleasant while others might be positively unpleasant. Perhaps it's the smell of perfume or aftershave, of car fumes and petrol, of food and drink, or fresh cut grass and plants. Notice how the mind habitually wants to create a story out of each of the smells, how it reminds you of somewhere, something or someone.

Finally, make a point of noticing any physical sensations or feelings. Perhaps it's the feeling of warm sunshine, cool rain or a cold breeze. Perhaps it's the sensation of the soles of the feet touching the ground with each step, or the weight of the arms swinging at your side, or even something painful like tight shoulders or that dodgy knee again. The intention is to simply acknowledge the sensations for thirty seconds or so, without feeling the need to get involved in thinking about the feelings.

As you continue to walk, don't try to prevent any of these things from entering your field of awareness – simply notice as they come and go, how one thing is constantly being replaced by the next. Think back to the road analogy, where the different-coloured cars are just coming and going, passing you by. The only difference is that you're now walking instead of sitting.

After a minute or two, gently shift your attention to the sensation of movement in the body. Notice how the weight shifts from the right side to the left side and then back again, usually in quite a steady rhythm. Try to avoid artificially adjusting your speed or trying to walk at a certain pace (unless you're somewhere quiet like a park or your own home). Instead, observe the way you walk and the rhythm you've become accustomed to. It may well be that as a result of doing this exercise you choose to walk a little more slowly in future.

Use the rhythm of the walking, the physical sensation of the soles of the feet touching the ground, as your base of awareness, a place you can mentally come back to once you realise the mind has wandered off. This is the equivalent of the rising and falling sensation of the breath when you do your sitting meditation.

There's no need to focus so intently that you start to exclude everything around you. In fact, be open to things happening around you and, when you know the mind has wandered off, just gently bring the attention back to the movement of the body and the sensation of the soles of the feet striking the ground each time.

Now because you'll be more present, more aware, it's quite likely that your mental habits (your usual ways of thinking) will also become more apparent. Usually, we're so caught up in the thoughts themselves, that we hardly notice our reactions to all these things. For example, how do you feel when the rhythm is broken by a red pedestrian light, and you are forced to stand and wait to resume walking? Is there a feeling of impatience, of wanting to move, to get on? Do you find yourself jockeying for position with other people? Or perhaps you might feel a sense of relief at the opportunity of being able to rest for a few seconds.

You might find it helpful to break this technique down into sections. For example, if you need to walk from A to B, and that walk is going to take ten or fifteen minutes, then it's best to do it on a street-by-street basis. At the beginning of each street, remind yourself of your intention to walk, free from distraction, until you reach the end of that street. As soon as you realise the mind has wandered off, just gently bring the attention back to the sensation on the soles of the feet. When you get to the end of that street, start again, as though it's a new exercise each time. This can make it feel much more manageable.

If you're fortunate enough to live close to a park, a river or some kind of pleasant outdoor space, then it's a good idea to try the technique in that environment too. There'll be much less external distraction in these areas, and this can change the way the exercise feels. It can also be useful in terms of knowing how your mind works differently in these contrasting environments.

Headspace for exercise

How often do you perform at the very best of your ability? Whether it's training in the gym to get fit, playing football with friends, jogging in the park, skiing down a mountain, doing yoga, swimming, cycling, or maybe even competing in a particular discipline, how often do you walk away thinking, 'Wow, that was great!' Of course, many people have a tendency to be self-critical, but even those people know when they've genuinely performed to the best of their ability. There's a feeling of having been 'in the zone' or 'in the moment', as if all the necessary conditions came together at just the right time to allow you to perform in that way. There's a sense of willing, of confidence, of focus. And the funny thing is, even if it's a really tough, physical session, it's almost as if there was an effortless quality about it. It's no coincidence that so many of these qualities are to be found in meditation.

If you watch professional athletes, performing at their very highest level, you'll notice that they spend a lot of time 'in the zone'. Sometimes they may slip in and out of it, but when they're truly performing at their best, it's as if nothing could disturb their focus. It's not an inward-looking focus, blocking out the sights and sounds around them. It's a focus that is perfectly balanced between an awareness of their own physicality and movement, and the changing environment around them. And it's not just the level of *focus* that seems to be perfectly balanced, so too is their level of *effort*. This doesn't mean they're applying maximum effort, but rather a *sustained naturalness* in which they appear to move gracefully and effortlessly. It's as though they are putting in much less effort than anyone else, and yet performing that much better.

Of course, it may be that these individuals have a natural ability for these sports. In fact, they unquestionably do. And it may well be that you're more interested in applying this technique to running on the treadmill at your local gym, than taking centre stage at Wimbledon. But a lot can be learnt about the relevance and role of meditation in sport by watching these individuals, especially when it comes to effort.

The image that best defines this for me is the slow motion shot you get as they replay the 100 metres sprint on television. You know the one, it's where you can see every part of their body moving around in far too much detail. Those runners at the front are usually very relaxed, very composed. Their cheeks wobble up and down and sway from side to side. In that moment they're the personification of the perfect mental balance between focus and relaxation. But if you look at those doing the chasing, they usually have very tight grimaces as they realise the race is getting away from them. The grimace is a response to that realisation, a tightening-up as they apply more effort. This is something to think about when you're applying mindfulness in everyday life. How much effort are you applying? Not to the 100 metres sprint, but to the simple things, opening and closing doors, wiping down a work surface, holding on to the steering wheel, turning off the tap, brushing your teeth. As you go about your day, start to notice just how much effort you put into these things. One thing is for sure, the level of effort you apply to life will almost certainly be reflected in your meditation.

The body and mind are not separate. When we have presence of mind we have presence of body, when we possess mental focus we possess physical focus, and when we have an ease of mind we have an ease of body. It sounds so obvious when we talk about it in those terms and yet how often do you apply any of those ideas to your exercise routine? It doesn't matter whether you're looking to improve your discipline, mental endurance, spatial awareness, concentration, pain management, or even your ability to perform under pressure, all of these factors rely on the mind. If your mind is present, alert and focused, yet with a sense of ease and relaxation, then you'll see progress, no question. If your mind is off thinking about a conversation you had yesterday, or wondering what you should buy your friend for their birthday next month, how can you possibly perform at your best? As with the walking meditation the great thing about this meditation is that it doesn't require you to take any additional time out of your day. Assuming you're already exercising in some way anyway, this will simply provide you with yet another opportunity to practise the art of being aware. And hey, if it improves your fitness or physical ability in the process, then that can't be a bad thing either.

The prostration

While training at one particular monastery, there was a very physical meditation technique that we had to do all day, every day, for about the first eight weeks of a one-year retreat. It involved going from a standing position, to a lying position, and then back to a standing position again. It's known as a prostration and is a skilful way of bringing together the body, speech and mind all at one time. It's usually done on a smooth surface, making it easier to push the hands out to a fully prone position when flat on the floor. To help with this further there are usually two pieces of material to place your hands on, making it easier to slide. Now at the same time as physically moving through that action, there's quite a long verse of Tibetan that needs to be repeated, which at times can feel like a bit of a tongue twister. This entire verse had to be repeated from memory and done quickly enough to match the physical movement of one prostration. Doing these two things alone was not unlike patting your head and rubbing your tummy in a circular motion at the same time. But there was more to come.

As part of the technique it was necessary to visualise quite a complicated image in the mind. It was a picture that involved lots of different people, sitting in various positions, wearing different clothes, holding different objects, all of which needed to be remembered and then visualised. This was at the same time as physically moving up and down from the floor and repeating the Tibetan verse over and over. In this way, the body, speech and mind all came together in perfect unison. At least that was the idea. When learning it was often the case that the body and speech would do as they should, almost habitually, but that the mind would wander off to think about other things. At other times it might be that the visualisation was very good, but that I'd suddenly notice that I was repeating absolute gibberish, not even remotely like the verse I'd rehearsed. And at times I'd be concentrating so hard on the *mental* aspect, that I'd not pay full attention to the physical movement and would fall flat on my face, which, when you're doing it at high speed, can really hurt.

The more I practised this technique, the more I started to see a pattern. If the balance of focus and relaxation was just right, then what was essentially a very physical exercise felt truly effortless. You could say that there was an equal amount of awareness in body, speech and mind. But if that balance was not right, one or two of those aspects would suffer as a result. At those times, far from feeling effortless, it was as though I was walking through treacle. And simply adding more effort didn't help at all. In fact, it only seemed to make it worse, even harder. As the weeks went by, I started to get a sense of how best to work with the mind on any given day – when to apply more effort, and when to ease my foot off the gas. And the mind became more willing too; it was getting used to this new way of focusing and was resisting a little less each day. Of course, the mind still wandered off sometimes, but it was easier to realise when it had, and to bring the attention back to the physical movement, the ability to speak coherently, and the visualisation of the image we'd studied. These changes seemed to coincide with me focusing less on the result, and more on simply being in the moment with each and every movement. If you can do the same thing with your favourite type of exercise, not only will you see big improvements in your performance, but you're also much more likely to do it with a greater sense of ease and enjoyment.

Don't be put off by the fact that it says 'running meditation' below if that's not your favourite kind of exercise. The principles are equally applicable to cycling, yoga, swimming, or any other sport for that matter. But as you've already been introduced to walking meditation, applying the principles to running will provide the most natural transition. There's no question that in terms of learning how to be mindful while exercising, it's much easier to do it with a form of exercise that has a repetitive nature and in which you are not directly competing with anyone else. So sports such as swimming, cycling, dance, running, golf, skiing, yoga and so on are perfect for this. While there's nothing wrong in starting off with games such as football, basketball, hockey and so on, there's a greater tendency to get sucked into your old habitual patterns, perhaps running around like a crazy thing and trying a little too hard.

In the same way that walking and eating have become very habitual for many people, so has running. This has its uses, as it means that it's easy to slip into a semi-conscious state of running, where the physical movement is so familiar that little concentration is required. Because of this, the mind tends to drift off very easily. So it's normal for the mind to wander when you're running, regardless of whether the thoughts are related to the running itself, or something quite separate. But the only way to ensure that you're performing to the very best of your ability, is to leave the thinking behind and allow the body and mind to work together with a combined physical and mental focus. You don't need to 'try not to think', but rather bring your attention to the process, rhythm and sensation of running. When you realise the mind has wandered off, just gently bring it back to the object of focus again.

Exercise 9: running meditation

This exercise is also available as a guided meditation at www.getsomeheadspace.com/headspace-book/get-some-headspace

Before you get ready to go out running, try to get a sense of how you're feeling . What's going on in the mind? Are you feeling anxious, confident, or perhaps completely indifferent? If you have the time and inclination, you can even take a couple of minutes to sit down and allow the mind to rest before you begin. If you do this each time you may start to notice a pattern that will help you to respond more skilfully.

As you get changed into your running clothes, begin to notice the physical sensations in the body. Perhaps the legs feel heavy from a previous run, or the shoulders tight from sitting at the computer. Or perhaps there's a general feeling of lightness in the body. As with the sitting technique, this process isn't done with any sense of judgment or analysis, you are simply building up an awareness of how you feel.

Before you leave, take a good few deep breaths. This will help you to focus and give you a greater sense of being grounded. Breathe in through the nose and out through the mouth. Once you're running you can return to whatever pattern of breathing feels most natural for you. Try to do this at least four or five times before you head out.

As you begin to run, at the same time as keeping a strong awareness of everything that's going on around you, bring your attention back to the body. How does it feel now that you're moving? How are the muscles responding to the movement? Notice how the breath quickly changes as the body begins to warm up. As always, there is nothing to do except be aware of all these things.

Notice how the mind responds too. Is it with a feeling of pleasure, of having 'got out' of work or home, of stretching your legs and getting some fresh air? Or is it a feeling of mild anxiety about the hard work you're expecting to experience later in the run? What about the thoughts? Is the mind very busy, churning up all the events of the day and looking ahead to the to-do list for tomorrow? Or does it feel very settled, perhaps even comforted by the physical movement?

As you settle into the run, begin to notice the rhythm you've established. Does it feel comfortable? How does the body feel? Does it feel balanced, with an equal amount of force being used in both legs? How do the arms feel? And the shoulders? Is there anywhere in the body that feels tight? If there is, you already know what to do with it – watch it, observe it, become aware of it. Resist the temptation to try and get rid of it somehow. You may well find that in the process of awareness, the tension naturally releases itself anyway.

If you're running for fun or simply to keep fit, then it's helpful to actively encourage an awareness of what's going on around you. This might be other runners, cars, parks, fields, buildings or anything else you pass along the way. It's amazing how often people run exactly the same route every day and yet how little they know about it, how little they actually see. And the only reason for this is the tendency to go inwards, to become lost in thought. So remember that idea of gentle curiosity, not frantically trying to notice everything around you, but being interested in the things that grab your attention.

Because you're more present and more aware, it's quite likely that the way you think when you run (your mental habits) will also become more apparent. Do you have a tendency to be hard or kind to yourself when you're running? Where does the mind instinctively go? Is it inwards towards thinking, or outwards towards sensations in the body? Is there a strong feeling of confidence, or of self-consciousness? All of these things you can start to notice as you do this exercise. You can also notice when the body begins to respond to the running process, when it releases the endorphins, when you start to feel invincible, as though you could run for ever (assuming that happens at some stage on your run).

One of the so-called problems of being more aware is that you become aware of not only the pleasant sensations, but also the unpleasant ones. However, used in the right way even the unpleasant sensations can be put to good effect. Rather than try to 'get away' from physical discomfort, see what happens when you rest your attention with the feeling. Try doing it as if you and the pain are not really separate, so less of 'me and my pain' and more of the simple, direct experience of 'pain'. The results might surprise you.

Whether it's the shortness of breath, the tightness of the chest, the aching of the thighs or cramping of the calves, all of these can be used as effective supports or objects of focus for your running meditation. When you first notice the pain, the instinctive reaction will be to resist it, to get rid of it, which will usually involve either stopping or beginning a long mental battle to try to forcibly overcome it, ignore it, or suppress it in some way. Obviously you need to be aware of your own physical capabilities, to respect your body, and take appropriate action when necessary. However, if you feel you can continue without doing any lasting damage, then try moving even closer to the discomfort, as if you are sinking down into that feeling and experiencing it in a very direct way. This may feel counterintuitive at first, but there's method to the madness. In moving closer to it, in fully experiencing it and even encouraging it, there's a complete shift in the usual, habitual dynamic and very often the pain is released as a result.

If you're running more seriously, perhaps even competitively, then you may prefer to focus purely on the process and mechanics of running. A useful and popular object of focus is the sensation of the foot striking the floor, similar to that of walking meditation. The sense of rhythm can be very relaxing and it's an obvious and stable point of focus.

Whatever your object of focus, try to run with a 'light touch' and relaxed mental attitude to the exercise. Even if you are pushing really hard to better your time, see just how little effort is required to run. Strange as that may sound, very often the more effort you put into it, the more you tighten up, and so the more you slow down. You could even make this the entire focus of your run, simply monitoring the amount of effort being applied. Notice in turn how this then affects your running stride.

Whether you are running for fun or taking it more seriously, you'll find this exercise far more manageable if you break it down into sections. Some people find that stride by stride is the best way to focus, whereas for others it is street by street, or even mile by mile. One popular method is to break down the run into every ten strides, or every twenty, or even every hundred. It's a bit like counting the breath and will help stop the mind wandering off. Obviously, the longer the distance you intend to focus on, the more difficult it is to remember these principles, so make a point of building in regular checks to see if you're present throughout the run.

Headspace for sleep

Have you ever wondered why it is that at the very moment your head hits the pillow at night, your thoughts seem to go into over-drive? I often hear this process being described as insomnia (because we like to give labels to things), but if it only happens every so often, then it's perhaps more accurate to describe it as being human. The interesting thing about this experience is that it's not always quite as it appears. Lying down in bed at night, free from all distractions, is not unlike the first few moments of meditation. Suddenly you're alone with your thoughts. All day you've been so busy with other people or doing other things, that these thoughts have been nothing but background noise in your head. While you may have had a vague awareness of this background noise, of thoughts coming and going, it's quite likely that many of them will have gone unacknowledged, unprocessed. Lying there undisturbed in the silence, it's only natural that those thoughts would become more obvious. It's a bit like the moment when you take off the blindfold in the road analogy I used earlier. So, is there anything you can do about this? The answer is most definitely yes, however it's useful to have a good understanding of the dynamic at work before you learn the exercise itself.

Let's say that you've had a busy day at work, come home, had a bite to eat and then watched a programme on television or been busy on the computer. While you might have felt fine watching television, engaged and distracted by what was on, having gone to bed you now suddenly feel very restless and agitated. Perhaps there's something specific on your mind, or perhaps it's simply the busy nature of the mind, the thoughts whizzing by, one after the next. Or maybe it's reflective of your lifestyle choices, irregular sleeping hours, jet-lag, or intake of stimulants. Whatever the reason, when the mind has built up a lot of momentum like this, it can take a little while for the thoughts to settle down. Of course we generally want them to settle immediately and when they don't, we inevitably end up feeling disappointed, frustrated, worried or upset. It's as if the more you try to shut the thoughts out, the more they seem to appear.

This isn't just your imagination working overtime, logic dictates that if you start thinking a lot about not being able to get to sleep, then you are by definition creating lots of additional thoughts. And by putting lots of effort into the process, you will at the same time be creating tension. In just the same way as meditation, the more you resist those thoughts and feelings, the more tension you create and this tension will be reflected and experienced in the body as well. It's usually at this point that the internal dialogue kicks in. 'I just can't get comfortable tonight . . . maybe I'll turn over and try on my other side . . . and I wonder why Harry said that today . . . did he mean something else? . . . maybe I should roll over . . . stop thinking, you need to get to sleep . . . oh no, my head's really busy again . . . why am I thinking so much? Oh it's so late . . . I'm never going to get to sleep . . . this feels just like last time when I couldn't sleep . . . and I felt terrible the next day . . . and I've got that really important meeting tomorrow . . . it's going to be a disaster . . . and I'm going to look terrible . . . why can't I just switch off these thoughts? OK, just relax, don't think about trying to go to sleep . . . but I can't stop . . . maybe I should get up . . . maybe I should read a book . . . stop thinking . . . oh why is my mind so busy?'

This may sound funny during the cold light of day, but when it's happening to us at night, the experience is anything but humorous. You may well feel angry at your inability to control the flow of thought, or scared that the thoughts will run away and lead to a sleepless night. You may feel depressed at the prospect of feeling tired the next day, or perhaps even worried that there's something wrong with you. These reactions are all quite normal and you're in no way alone in your experience. It stands to reason that the busier and more stressed you are during the day, the more likely this situation will occur at night, but it can sometimes become a habit quite separate from the affairs of day-to-day living. Whichever it is, the fact that it's behavioural rather than physiological (and I'm assuming this is something you will have clarified with your GP if you have serious concerns) means that it can change. And it can change in one of two ways. Either the habit of resistance is 'unlearned', or a new, more positive way of relating to the thoughts and feelings is adopted. I've experienced both over the years, and there was one situation in particular when this technique proved invaluable.

The Russian policemen

Turning up at the airport in Moscow, I didn't really know what to expect. I'd heard a lot of things about the city, and about Russia in general, but I didn't really know how much to believe. It was just at the time that residential apartment blocks in different parts of the city were being randomly targeted and blown up in the middle of the night. The Russian government accused the Chechens of terrorism, and the Chechen government accused the Russians of conspiring to create the grounds for invading their territory in the south of the country. Needless to say, there was a palpable sense of anxiety in the air. People had started to look at their neighbours in a different way, especially if they were foreign or from another part of Russia. It wasn't so much that everyone was a suspect, but more that everyone felt a certain responsibility to look out for any strange activity. Back in the Soviet days, every apartment block had a 'babushka', an elderly woman who would sit at the front of the building and monitor all the activity within it. During the apartment block bombings, this tradition was fully resurrected in all buildings, with the babushkas keeping an eye out and reporting anything unusual to the police.

Having arrived late in the evening, the lady who'd met me at the airport dropped me off at the flat and arranged to meet me the next morning. I didn't even notice the elderly woman peeking out of her front window as I walked up the stairs. I was too tired to do anything much when I got to the flat, but unpacked a few very simple items. It had become a bit of a ritual for me that wherever I travelled, the first thing I would do was set up a small area for meditation. I guess it just reflected the priority I gave to it at that time. So I wiped down the surface of a shelf, took out a few simple objects, a couple of pictures of my teachers, and placed my meditation cushion on the floor in front of it. Realising I would fall asleep if I sat to meditate then and there, I decided to go to bed and get up first thing in the morning and do it then instead. So, leaving the rest of my stuff in the suitcase, and not even taking the time to make my bed, I simply took off my clothes and fell asleep.

Time is a funny thing. It's hard to say whether I'd been asleep for five minutes or five hours, but I was awoken by a group of men shouting and banging loudly on my front door. Feeling sleepy and not altogether sure where I was, I stumbled towards the door. I was so tired that I didn't even think about the fact that I was dressed only in my underwear. Nor did I think about checking the peephole in the door to see who was standing on the other side. I just walked to the door, unlocked the deadbolt, opened it and . . . suddenly woke up, very, very quickly. Facing me were four policemen, holding very big guns and shouting loudly as they moved towards me into the flat. I didn't understand a word they were saying and apparently none of them spoke English either. They were clearly excited about something or other – and not in a good way. Three of them moved from one room to the next, looking in cupboards, searching through my suitcase, as one stayed with me, blocking my exit to the front door with his gun.

Having satisfied themselves that the apartment was not packed full of explosives, as had been intimated to them by the babushka on the door, everyone started to relax a little. But only a little. They continued to talk loudly and forcefully. I glanced at the clock. It was only 12.30 a.m., so I'd been asleep for less than half an hour before they arrived, although I could have sworn it was longer. They asked me for my passport, my documents, my work papers and one by one sat down at the dining room table to examine them. I remained standing, still dressed in nothing more than my green underpants. 'So,' I thought to myself, 'what do you do when someone comes to your home and takes a seat at your table? Well, I guess you offer them a cup of tea.' Fortunately, a few basic provisions had been left for me and so, still under the watch of one of the four policemen, I went into the kitchen and hurriedly made the tea. As I came back, one of the policemen noticed the area I'd set up for meditation. 'Ah,' he said, 'Karate, da?', gesturing to make clear his suggestion. Not knowing how to say, 'Well actually, no, this is where I'm planning to sit and do my meditation when I don't have policemen with guns running around the place', I smiled politely and nodded my head.

This seemed to please the men a lot. They started to laugh and joke among themselves. Whether they were laughing *at* me or *with* me is hard to say. Just to see them laughing was good enough. They then started to point at different things, clearly trying to ask a question. One of them even pointed at my pants, which was a little disconcerting, given I had no idea what they were asking. It took a little while, but I eventually established that they were trying to ask what colour belt I was in karate, what standard I'd reached. Riding the wave of laughter, I jokingly pointed at the chair, which was black. This really seemed to get them excited and they started to gesture for me to demonstrate. I tried to explain that I'd been joking, but they didn't understand. So a game of semi-naked charades began where I tried to indicate I was too tired, it had been a long flight, and so on. Eventually the men gave up, realising that there would be no brick smashing or door breaking on this occasion, and left me alone to go back to bed.

'Welcome to Russia' I thought to myself as I lay back down. It was now after 1 a.m., but I was wide awake. My mind was racing with thoughts and my body was still pumping with adrenaline. I knew I was tired and needed the sleep, but I had no idea how it was ever going to happen. Thoughts of the police, the apartment bombings and my new life in Russia filled my mind. I was also conscious of the fact that early the next morning I would be meeting lots of new people who I'd be working with in the months to come and, let's face it, first impressions count for a lot. So I lay there with all these thoughts buzzing around. Now if I'd faced this kind of situation before I'd received any training in meditation, I'm certain I'd have been awake for the rest of the night. But having been shown a way to deal with the situation, the mind started to calm down surprisingly quickly.

The more I was able to simply watch the thoughts, to be aware of them as they passed through the mind, the more the mind seemed to quieten. As the mind settled down, so the body began to feel less agitated. Knowing that no amount of effort was going to force me back to sleep, I let the metaphorical rope out a bit and allowed the mind lots of space. It can be helpful to think back to some of the analogies here, whether it's taming the wild horse, the idea of the blue sky and the thoughts passing by as clouds, or any other one of them that you might find helpful in increasing your sense of perspective and space. For me it was the blue sky. But old habits can sometimes be very strong and every now and then I'd notice that I'd slipped into trying really hard again. But as soon as I became aware of the effort being applied, it was as if it suddenly vanished. It came back again of course, but it was the same thing each time, as long as I was aware of the effort then it never really seemed to build up any momentum. Soon enough I started to feel sleepy again and I eventually dozed off for the night.

This exercise I'm about to show you is applicable to all forms of sleeplessness, whether that's being unable to go to sleep, waking frequently throughout the night, or waking very early in the morning and being unable to go back to sleep. It's even applicable if you're not experiencing any of the above, but simply want to know how to experience a more restful sleep, or wake without feeling groggy in the morning. Although this particular exercise is designed to be done in the evening, in bed, immediately before you go to sleep, it's not meant as a replacement for Take10. In fact, you'll find that doing Take10 on a daily basis, at the same time as learning this exercise, is the best combination.

Many people find that their sleep improves simply as a result of doing Take10. This is without doing any particular techniques at night in bed. And the scientific research seems to back this up. Most of the trials that have been done to assess the benefits of meditation and mindfulness on insomnia have requested participants to practise the technique during the day rather than at night, with equally impressive results. So it might be more useful to think of this in terms of having a healthy mind over a twenty-four-hour period, rather than exclusively targeting your mind at night.

The exercise below is designed to take about fifteen to twenty minutes, although obviously it doesn't matter if you fall asleep halfway through. In fact, it's very normal to fall asleep and this in no way detracts from the long-term benefits of the exercise. Remember, this is not an exercise to *make* you go to sleep, but rather to increase your awareness and understanding of your mind at night. It just so happens that it often results in sleep. You'll probably find it much more comfortable to download the audio of the exercise and be guided through the process, but within a few nights you'll be familiar and confident enough with each section to do it without the guided version if you prefer.

Exercise 10: sleeping meditation

This exercise is also available as a guided meditation at www.getsomeheadspace.com/headspace-book/get-some-headspace

Before going to bed, make sure you've been to the bathroom, locked the door, turned off your phone and done all the other things you usually do before going to bed. If you find it helps, you could even prepare a few things for the morning or make a list of things you need to do the next day.

Having got ready for bed, lie flat on your back under the covers, as if you were about to go to sleep. If you find it more comfortable, place a thin pillow under your head. It doesn't matter if you usually sleep on your front or side, this exercise is best done lying on your back and you can always flip over afterwards. As you lie there, take a moment to appreciate the sensation of sinking into the bed, the feeling that your body is being supported and that you have reached the end of the day, with nothing more to do.

Once you're lying comfortably, take five deep breaths, breathing in through the nose and out through the mouth, just as you do in the core technique. As you breathe in, try to get a sense of the lungs filling with air and the chest expanding. As you breathe out, imagine the thoughts and feelings of the day just disappearing into the distance, and any feelings of tension in the body just melting away. This will help to prepare both the body and the mind for the exercise ahead.

Step 1: Begin by checking-in, in the usual way, noticing how you're feeling, in both body and mind. Remember that in the same way you can't rush relaxation, neither can you rush sleep, so take your time with this part of the exercise. Don't worry if there are lots of thoughts whizzing around (this is absolutely normal) and for now just let them do their own thing. Whatever you do, avoid the temptation to resist the thoughts, no matter how unsettling or uncomfortable they may be.

Next become aware of the physical points of contact in a little bit more detail. Bring your attention back to the sensation of the body touching the bed, the weight of the body sinking down into the mattress. Notice where the points of contact are strongest – is the weight distributed evenly? You can also notice any sounds or other sensations. Sounds can be especially disturbing when you're trying to go to sleep. At first it's helpful to recognise whether it's a sound you can change, or if it's something outside of your control, something you can do nothing about. Then, rather than resisting the sound, gently rest your attention on it, remaining present with the sound for thirty seconds or so, before bringing your attention back to the body.

Now try to get a sense of how the body actually feels. At first, do this in a general way. For example, does the body feel heavy or light, restless or still? Then try to get a more accurate picture by mentally scanning down through the body, from head to toe, gently observing any tension or tightness. Invariably the mind will be drawn to any areas of tension, but you can relax in the knowledge that you are about to sleep and that the exercise will help to release those areas. You can do this scan several times, taking about twenty to thirty seconds each time. Remember to notice the areas that feel relaxed and comfortable, as well as any areas of discomfort.

By now you will have probably already noticed the rising and falling sensation of the breath, but if you haven't, just bring your attention to that place in the body where you feel the movement most clearly. As always, don't try to change the rhythm of the breath in any way, instead allow the body to do its own thing. As with Take10, there is no right or wrong way to breathe within the context of this exercise, so don't worry if you feel it more in the chest than the stomach. Notice whether the breath is deep or shallow, long or short, smooth or irregular. This doesn't require very much effort at all. All you need to do is to be aware of the movement.

If the breath is very shallow and hard to detect, you might find it helpful to place your hand on whichever part of the body you feel the strongest movement. And as it rests there, trace the rise and fall as your hand moves back and forth.

As you watch the breath for a minute or two, it's quite normal for the mind to wander off. When you realise you've been distracted, that the mind has wandered off, in that moment you are back in the present, and all you need do is gently return the focus to the rising and falling sensation. You don't need to time this part of the exercise, you can just naturally move on to the next section when it feels as if a couple of minutes has passed.

Step 2: This next part of the exercise is about thinking back through the day in a focused and structured way. Begin by thinking back to the very first moment you can remember in the day, right after waking up in the morning. Do you remember how you felt upon waking? Now, as if your brain has been set to a very gentle 'fast-forward', simply watch as your mind replays the events, meetings and conversations of the day. This doesn't need to be in detail, it's more of an overview, a series of snapshots passing through the mind.

For example, picture yourself rolling out of bed, turning off the alarm, walking to the bathroom, having a shower, eating your breakfast, doing your meditation, walking to work, greeting a colleague and so on. Take about three minutes to go through the entire day, right up to the present moment. It might seem like a lot to fit into just a few minutes, but as I say, this is only an overview of the day, so don't take any longer than three or four minutes. After a couple of days you'll no doubt feel comfortable with the speed of it.

As the mind replays the day, there is the inevitable temptation to jump in and get caught up in the thinking. Perhaps it was a meeting that went really well and you start to think about all the potential possibilities. Or perhaps it was an argument with your boss, and you start to worry about the implications of the discussion. It's normal for the mind to wander like this at first, but obviously it's not helpful to get involved in new thinking at this time of night. So, as before, when you realise you've been distracted, gently return to the film playing back in your mind and pick up where you left off.

Step 3: Having brought yourself up to the present moment, you can now return your focus to the body. Place your attention on the small toe of the left foot and imagine that you're just switching it off for the night. You can even repeat the words 'switch off' or 'and rest' in your mind as you focus on the toe. It's as if you're giving the muscles, joints, bones and everything else permission to switch off for the night, knowing they will not be needed again until the morning. Do the same with the next toe, and the next, and so on. Continue in this way through the ball of the foot, the arch, the heel, the ankle, the lower half of the leg and so on all the way up to the hip and pelvic area.

Before you repeat this exercise with the right leg, take a moment to notice the difference in the feeling between the leg that has been 'switched off' and the one that hasn't. If there was any doubt in your mind about whether anything was actually happening as you do this exercise, you'll feel it now. Repeat the same exercise on the right leg, once again starting with the toes and working your way all the way up to the waist.

Continue this exercise up through the torso, down through the arms, hands and fingers, and up through the throat, neck, face and head. Take a moment to enjoy the sensation of being free of tension, of not needing to do anything with the body, of having given up control. You can now allow the mind to wander as much as it wants, freely associating from one thought to the next, no matter where it wants to go, until you drift off to sleep.*

Optional extra: It's quite possible that by the time you've reached this point in the exercise you will be fast asleep. If you are, enjoy the rest and sleep well. Don't worry if you're not asleep though – it's not that you've done the exercise incorrectly. Remember that it's not an exercise to *make* you go to sleep, but rather an exercise to increase your awareness and understanding of your mind at night.

So, if you're still awake, there are two ways to go. The first is to allow the mind to drift off, in the usual way, freely associating as it wants, without any sense of control or coercion on your behalf. This can feel very nice, but the only problem is that for some it feels a little vague or even disconcerting. If that's the case for you, then this final part of the exercise will be a more helpful way to conclude.

Begin by counting backwards from 1,000 to zero. This may sound like an impossible task, and a bit too much like hard work. But done in the right way it takes no effort at all. And it's a great way to keep the mind focused as you make the transition to sleep. As before, it's quite normal for the mind to wander, so when you realise you've become distracted, just gently return to whichever number you left off and pick it up from there.

As a final note, it's important that you do this exercise with the genuine wish to reach zero. Do not think of it as a way of getting to sleep, but as an exercise to keep you occupied and focused until your body and mind are ready to switch off for the night. No matter what thoughts arise in the mind, whether they're about going to sleep or otherwise, simply allow them to come and go. Your only intention, your only focus, is to try and make it to zero. And if you should drift off to sleep midway in the process, then that's fine too.

What the research shows

1 Meditation related to self control

Researchers investigating the effectiveness of mindfulness found that after just ficve days of meditating for a very short time, participants showed increased blood flow to the area of the brain that helps to control emotions and behaviour. After eleven hours of meditation had been completed, actual physical changes in this part of the brain had occurred. Perhaps unsurprisingly then, in preliminary studies mindfulness has been shown to be effective in the treatment of drug addiction, smoking and eating disorders. In one such study, binge eating decreased by over 50% in just forty-two days.

2 Mindfulness improves performance under stress

Neuroscientists at the University of Pennsylvania investigated whether mindfulness could help offset the loss of mental perform-ance of Marines in stressful situations. In the words of the lead researcher, 'Building mind-fitness with mindfulness training can help anyone who must maintain peak performance in the face of extremely stressful circumstances, from first responders, relief workers and trauma surgeons, to professional and Olympic athletes.'

3 Meditation can halve the time it takes to get to sleep

Researchers from the University of Massachusetts Medical School developed an effective approach to sleep which incorporated meditation as an integral component. The study found that 58% of diagnosed insomniacs reported significant improvements and 91% of those using medication either reduced their dose or stopped taking it completely. In a separate, but related study at Stanford

Medical Centre, neuroscientists discovered that, after just six weeks of mindfulness, participants were able to fall asleep in half the time than usual – averaging twenty minutes instead of forty minutes.

4 Mindfulness can help you to meet that deadline

In several mindfulness-based studies, researchers have found that practitioners showed significant improvements in their cognitive skills after only four days of training. They performed particularly well on physical and mental tasks requiring sustained attention – and also in stressful tasks performed under time constraints. I'll leave it up to the experts of just one of those studies to give you their verdict: 'The meditation group did especially better on all the cognitive tests that were timed ... In tasks where participants had to process information under time constraints causing stress, the group that briefly trained in mindfulness performed significantly better.'

5 Meditation keeps you bright and alert

Researchers at Emory University in the US set about comparing the brains and cognitive skills of meditators to a similar group of non-meditators. In the control group they found that the older participants had lower accuracy and speed of response, as you might expect. However, this age-related decline was not found in the meditators. Using sophisticated brain-mapping techniques they discovered that the reduction in grey matter that typically comes with aging had actually been offset by the meditation.

Practicalities

I've said it before, but it's worth repeating: meditation only works if you do it! It's only when you sit down and do it on a regular basis that you'll see any benefit. So while the practice of mindfulness can be applied any time, any place, anywhere, there's no substitute for a daily meditation session. Those ten minutes will give you the very best opportunity and conditions to become familiar with what it means to be aware. It's also likely to provide you with a sense of stillness which is very difficult to replicate in everyday life when you first begin. So, whether you think of it as an isolated exercise to get some headspace, the foundations for practising mindfulness throughout the day, or simply as a new hobby, the importance of sitting down to do it daily cannot be overstated.

It doesn't matter whether your mind is currently busy or quiet, happy or sad, stressed or relaxed. All of these mind states are appropriate starting points for meditation. What matters is whether you are able to rest in awareness of that mind state, with a sense of ease. And this is something that can only be done through consistent, regular practice. And it is this experience that has the potential to fundamentally transform your perspective of life.

Remember, we're only talking about ten minutes of your day. There are truly very few people in the world who don't have ten minutes to spare in the day. This is not work, some additional chore (although, strangely, people often perceive it that way), these ten minutes are your time to relax. They are probably the only ten minutes in your entire day when you have absolutely nothing to do at all except be aware. How could that be considered a chore? We're so used to doing *something* that we find the idea of doing *nothing* somewhat alien or boring at first. You don't need to think of meditation as 'working on yourself', it's simply ten minutes out of your day to allow the body and mind to unwind, while becoming more familiar with the idea of being present, of being aware.

Before we come to the practicalities of your practice, there are a couple of points that can't be avoided. I said at the beginning that this book wasn't about telling you how to live your life, and this remains the case. How you choose to live your life is up to you. It may be that as a result of practising meditation you decide to make a few positive changes in your life, and that's your choice. But meditation and mindfulness are not something separate from the rest of life. The mind goes with us wherever we go. Even if you run away to a mountaintop in the Himalayas, your mind will still be there with you (I can vouch for it). So if our meditation reflects our everyday state of mind, then how we live our life is going to have a significant impact on our meditation.

With that in mind, it makes sense to increase those aspects of life that promote wellbeing, and decrease those aspects that might cause guilt, fear, regret, anger and the like.

The comparison of training at the gym is a useful one. You may be diligently going every day and feeling pretty good about it, then a trainer suggests that you could see even more benefits if you eased up on the family-sized portions of deep fried chicken for lunch every day. And so it is with meditation. I know from my own experience that how I choose to live is reflected in my practice. If I treat someone badly, then when I sit down to do my meditation my mind will experience an unusually high volume of challenging thoughts. Likewise, if I go out and get hammered after work, there's a good chance that the same session will descend into a drunken sleep. Neither approach provides conducive conditions for being aware, to experience more calm or more clarity.

And there's little point in training your mind if you neglect the wellbeing of your body. Most people respond very well to some kind of physical activity or exercise each day (even those who are not terribly enthusiastic about the idea). In fact many people say that their ability to apply just the right amount of effort to their meditation is even enhanced in some way when they do some exercise first. It doesn't have to be yoga, but it's fine if it is. It can be anything, but preferably something you enjoy. Similarly, ask yourself how certain foods make you feel. Do you find that some help you to feel vital and alive, whereas others leave you feeling agitated or sleepy? Investigate these areas, take the time to notice what aspects of your life seem to improve the quality of headspace, and which aspects detract from it.

Here are just a few of the practicalities that will help you to establish a fruitful and regular meditation practice. You'll find lots more useful advice on our website at www.getsomeheadspace.com.

Finding the right place

Few of us have the luxury of our own meditation room, but fortunately you can learn to meditate just about anywhere. There are a few useful things to bear in mind when you start. Find a place where you can sit, undisturbed, for ten minutes. This is easier said than done in some family homes, so it's important you communicate this requirement with your family. If there's nobody else around to look after young children, then you may need to wait for them to go to sleep before you begin, or practise before they wake in the morning. When you're starting out it's important to have that space, those brief ten minutes, to yourself if you can. People often worry about the amount of external noise, but as I mentioned earlier, this need not be a concern and can be incorporated into the exercise. That said, if you have the choice between a noisy environment and a quiet environment, opt for the latter.

You may like to use the same space each day. There's something useful in doing this in terms of reaffirming the new habit. There's also something comforting about returning to that same place each day. You may find it more relaxing if the space is relatively tidy too. Think back to the last time you walked into a very messy room, or a very tidy room. How did they make you feel? Did the tidy room bring about a sense of calm? For many people it will do, so if that's the case for you then you might like to keep that room, or at least that area of the room, clear and tidy.

Finally, while you can position yourself anywhere you like in the room, you might find it more comfortable to have some space around you. When you are wedged into a corner, or stuck between two pieces of furniture, it can sometimes feel a little cramped, which is not so good for the mind. Meditation can be done anywhere. In fact, I know several people who have resorted to doing it while sitting on the toilet (with the lid down) as this is the only space they can find where they'll be undisturbed.

What to wear

It doesn't really matter what you wear to meditate, so long as you're comfortable. That's just one of the many things that makes meditation so flexible. You can do it on the way to work in a suit, at home in your jogging suit, or even in your pyjamas. However, there are a couple of tips for clothing that you might find useful. Probably the most important is having enough room to breathe. It's no good sitting to relax if your jeans are so tight that the stomach can't move, so make sure to loosen any belts or even to undo a button or two if necessary. It's also helpful to have your feet placed firmly on the ground, so make sure you take off any heels if you're wearing any. You don't need to do it barefoot (although that's fine if you want to), but you'll probably feel more grounded if the feet are flat on the floor and it will make the first part of the exercise easier to do too. Finally, if you're wearing a tie or a scarf then you might like to loosen it. Feeling any sense of restriction can be off-putting as you sit there, so make sure you do everything you need to do to make yourself comfortable.

How to sit

First and foremost, it's what you do with your mind rather than what you do with your body that is most important. The body plays a part too, but as I've said, there's nothing special about being able to sit in a perfect lotus position on the floor if your mind is all over the place. If you are considering taking up meditation as a full-time career, then there are some benefits in learning to sit in the traditional way. But for the purposes of a daily practice, it's perfectly acceptable to use a chair. Having trained in one particular monastery, where all our meditation was done sitting on chairs, I can assure you that meditation works every bit as well in this way. The important thing is to be comfortable, relaxed and at ease, but with a feeling of being focused and alert at the same time.

Take a moment to think how the body reflects the mind. If we're very tired, or feel a bit lazy, then we tend to lie down. If we're energetic or speedy, we might need to keep active. If we feel angry our bodies generally get tighter. On the other hand, if we feel very relaxed, the body tends to feel a bit looser. This feedback loop is worth remembering when you sit to meditate each day. You are looking to take up a position on the chair that is stable, confident and alert, and yet at the same time that is relaxed and at ease. By adopting a physical posture that reflects the qualities of mind you'd like to develop, it will make it that much easier to do so.

Any chair can be used for this purpose, but you might find it easier to use an upright kitchen or dining room-style chair. Armchairs and sofas, and most definitely beds, are all a little too soft and spongy for this purpose. They might give you the feeling of relaxation, but are unlikely to give you the feeling of being alert. So a chair that encourages just a little bit of effort to maintain your posture might be best. There are a few general suggestions for sitting:

1 It's best if the back is straight, but without forcing it.
2 You may find that the position of your pelvis dictates the position of your back, and often a small cushion under your backside will help to rectify any 'hunching'.
3 It's fine to use the chair's back support if you need to, but try not to lean backwards against it – think upwards rather than backwards.
4 It's best if your legs are uncrossed and your feet are flat on the floor, ideally about shoulder width apart.

5 The hands and the arms can just rest on the legs or in your lap, one on top of the other. There's no need at all to make any special shapes with your fingers, as you may have seen in some pictures in the past, instead just allow the full weight of your fingers, hands and arms to be supported by the legs.

6 As obvious as it may sound, it's good if the head can be balanced reasonably straight on top of your neck, neither looking up into the air, or slumped down towards the floor. Not only will you find this more comfortable, but you'll also find that it improves your ability to concentrate.

7 Lastly, you'll probably want to close your eyes at first, as it reduces the amount of distraction. All of this is explained in more detail in the section that introduces you to Take10.

Finding the right time in the day

There are a few things you might like to consider before committing to a particular time of day to take your ten minutes. Perhaps you tend to wake feeling groggy in the morning, or are always in such a rush that you can't imagine doing it first thing. Or perhaps you get very tired towards the end of the day and know that meditation will inevitably end in sleep if you leave it until the evening. Maybe you have a quiet space at work that you are already eyeing up, thinking you could perhaps squeeze it in at lunchtime. We're all very different and it's important that you find a time that is comfortable for you and that works for you. However, there's one time to avoid if you can, and that's straight after lunch. The body tends to feel very heavy around this time of day, busy with the digestion process, and it is all too easy to fall asleep. This can be the same after a heavy evening meal too.

I'm often asked what I would recommend as the best possible time of the day, and I always answer the same way. No matter whether you are a lark or an owl, the best time of the day to do your meditation when you are learning is first thing in the morning. One of the most practical reasons for this is that it tends to be a quiet time of day, when other people in the house are still asleep, so it's easier to find a quiet spot to sit undisturbed. It's also an opportunity to allow the grogginess of the night to clear away, leaving you refreshed and in a good state of mind to approach the day ahead. But probably the most important reason is that if you do it in the morning, it gets done. Leaving it until later in the day can be a dangerous strategy as other commitments, deadlines or interruptions crop up. And if you leave it until you get home from work, you may well feel as though you just want to slump on the sofa, as if even the idea of meditation seems too much. In fact, I've even known people get stressed about trying to fit in their meditation. It keeps getting added to the next 'to do' list, only to be 'not done'. So the very thing that they set out to learn to reduce their stress has somehow become a further source of stress. This is not the way it was intended!

The idea of finding time early in the morning can be daunting. But keep in mind that we are still only talking about ten minutes. And this is ten minutes that is going to set up your entire day for you. We may feel desperate for more sleep, but the deep rest experienced in meditation is far more useful and beneficial than the extra ten minutes of sleep you would otherwise get. What's more, you're conscious of it.

It's for you to decide when is best, but give yourself the best chance to make this work by choosing a time that is realistic, when you know that you'll be able to do it on a daily basis.

Measuring time

Many people say they feel that setting a timer is the very antithesis of meditation. 'How can you get any headspace when you are under pressure to do it in a set period of time?' But this is maybe not the most helpful way of looking at it. There are practical reasons for using a timer. It's not uncommon to fall asleep during meditation and so it's important you're woken up when you originally intended to finish (especially if you need to be at work on time). There's also the issue of knowing how long you've been sitting there for – sometimes a minute can feel like ten minutes, and at other times vice versa. But there's one final reason which is perhaps the most important of all.

When it comes to meditation, every day is different. One day you might find that your mind is very quiet, at other times it might be very busy. Sometimes there may be no particular emotion around, whereas at other times you might feel an emotion very intensely. Now when you feel calm and relaxed I've no doubt that you'll be able to sit and meditate comfortably for ten minutes. In fact, you may even decide, after sitting for ten minutes, that you're enjoying it so much, you're going to make it a twenty minute session instead. In contrast, if your mind is busy and you feel irritated about something, you may well find that after just a couple of minutes you think there's no point in continuing and decide to quit there and then.

If the purpose of meditation is to know one's own mind, then with this approach you'll only ever get to know the happy and calm aspects of the mind, and never the more troublesome aspects. This may sound quite appealing at first, but when was the last time you had a problem with feeling too happy or too relaxed? So it's the troublesome thoughts and emotions that we need to get to know the best. In order to know your own mind, and therefore experience life with a renewed sense of perspective, it's important to always cross the finishing line, to complete the ten minutes, no matter what. By the same measure, on those days when you're feeling great, as though you could continue for ever, it's best if you stop when the timer goes off. This way you'll develop a very honest and useful practice. Of course, if you want to repeat the exercise later in the day, then do, but continue to follow the same ten minute rule to begin with.

As a final note, try to find a timer that is not going to make you jump when it goes off. One man I know bought a cooking timer for this purpose and then experienced heart palpitations every time it went off. You might find a nice gentle alarm on your mobile phone. Just ensure that the phone is turned over so that you can't see the screen, that it's switched on to silent, and that the vibrate function is also switched off. The temptation to look to see who has just called or texted might just be a little too much to resist if you don't do those three things first. You might also like to choose an alarm that is different to the one you use to wake up to in the morning. People have particular associations and even strong feelings of aversion to that sound, so it might be best not to make it part of your daily meditation.

The importance of repetition

Meditation is a skill and, like any skill, needs to be repeated on a regular basis if it's to be learnt and refined. There is something about the momentum that builds up when you sit to do it every day which simply cannot be replicated. It's the same when starting a new exercise programme. It requires a regular commitment to build up enough momentum for it to become part of your daily routine, almost without needing to think about it. By doing it at the same time each day, it helps you to develop a very strong and stable practice.

Neuroscientists investigating the benefits of meditation and mindfulness reiterate the importance of repetition in their findings. They say that the simple act of doing the exercise day after day is enough to stimulate positive change in the brain. In fact, they consider this vital in establishing new synaptic relationships and neural pathways. What this means is that new patterns of behaviour and mental activity can be created and, just as importantly, old patterns of mental activity can be let go of. As so much of our mental activity is habitual, the implications of this are nothing short of life changing. The research also showed that it didn't even matter whether the experience was perceived as positive or negative by the meditator, the same beneficial effects in the brain were still recorded. So even when it feels as though it might not be going so well, something positive is happening. No matter how you might feel on any particular day, try to repeat the process, for it's through this repetition the foundations are laid for more headspace in the future.

If you do miss a day once in a while, don't let that be the reason to give up meditation altogether. Use it as an opportunity to strengthen your resolve, to practise your resilience, and to be adaptive to changing circumstances. You will still see benefits. As a client recently remarked, 'It's hard to say exactly what the benefits are. All I know is that on the days I do it I feel great, and on the days I don't do it, I feel rubbish.' Start to notice how you feel when you do it, and also how you feel when you are forced to miss it for some reason.

Remembering to remember

People often say to me that while they appreciate the concept of remaining mindful throughout the day, or even stopping to take out ten minutes for a meditation exercise, they find it hard to remember to do it. For one reason or another the day just seems to pass them by and before they know it they are lying in bed, just getting ready to fall asleep, when they suddenly remember that they forgot. Then they feel guilty about not doing it, assume that they are hopeless, and decide that maybe meditation is not for them. Before you go down that route, here are a few things to consider.

Part of the skill in learning meditation is remembering to do it, being conscious enough, awake enough, to realise that now is the time that you have put aside to practise. Don't be surprised if you forget a few times to begin with, it's quite normal to do so. But it underlines the importance of having a set time of day when you always do it. My guess is you rarely forget to brush your teeth or have a shower in the morning, or to eat your dinner and watch your favourite television programme in the evening, right?

Taking ten minutes can be achieved by finding that same slot in the day's schedule, but remembering to be mindful throughout the day can be a little more challenging. In fact, at Headspace events we even hand out small round stickers for people to put on their phones, computers, cupboard doors and so on, to remind themselves to be mindful and aware throughout the day. There's nothing on the sticker, so it doesn't mean anything to anyone else, but to those people it's a reminder to be present. If you think it might help, you could do something similar to help you remember.

Trusting your own experience

The thing with meditation is that it's difficult to quantify or judge. As I mentioned earlier, there really is no such thing as good or bad meditation, just aware or unaware, distracted or undistracted. So if you were to judge it would have to be on that basis. But don't feel you have to rate it compared to another session or, even worse, against someone else's experience – meditation is just what it is.

Trust your own experience and don't just rely on other people's opinions. This is part of making meditation a practical reality in your life. To paraphrase one very famous meditation teacher, don't just do it because I say it works. Try it for yourself and see if it makes a difference for you. Do it consistently and honestly and be the judge of whether it made any difference. If it did, you'll have a little more confidence in continuing to do it and perhaps even doing it for a little longer each day. If it doesn't seem to make a difference, give it some more time. Doing it just once or twice is like switching on the kettle when you are trying out some new coffee. You need to at least wait for the kettle to boil, to pour out the water and taste the coffee, before you can really say whether it works for you or not. This is why I usually recommend doing it for a very minimum of ten days before you completely rule it out.

What to do if you feel uncomfortable or agitated

It's very common to feel slightly agitated or restless when you first sit down to meditate and it's useful to think back to the analogy of the wild horse in these situations. If you've been busy doing other things, or have simply been thinking a lot, the mind is unlikely to immediately sit still. It will have built up a certain amount of momentum that will take a few minutes to settle down again, and it's only natural to experience that movement of mind physically as well as mentally. So remember the idea of giving the mind space and allowing it to come to a natural place of rest in its own time, just as I described earlier.

As you move towards the end of your meditation session (no matter how long you are sitting for) you might begin to experience some discomfort. You might notice how this happens on one day and yet not on another, and it's worth being aware of these changes and looking to see if the physical pain reflects the state of the mind in any way. You might also like to refer back to 'The Reversal' story on page 50 as this is a great way of dealing with discomfort of any kind. Now unless you have a severe back problem, then sitting in a chair for a short while should present no real physiological challenges. That said, for most people it is quite unusual to sit still without any distractions and so inevitably you will become aware of little niggles and discomfort in the body that you wouldn't usually notice. The important thing to remember is that those areas of discomfort were already there before you sat down. All the meditation has done is shine a light of awareness on them so you can see them more clearly. At first this sounds like bad news, but in fact it's actually very good news because we need to see these things clearly before we can let go of them. So it's almost as though by witnessing the discomfort coming to the surface, you are witnessing its departure. Needless to say, if you experience chronic or acute pain of any kind it is best to check it out with your doctor. But whatever you do, don't let mild discomfort be an excuse not to meditate because you just never know when headspace might strike.

Recording your feedback

Whether it's through the forum on our Facebook bookpage (check out www.facebook.com/HeadspaceOfficial), or in the diary at the back of this book, it can be really helpful to record your experience of meditation when you start out. Otherwise the experience can quickly be lost and mixed up with other feelings both before and after the meditation. This is not about judging in a 'marks out of ten' way, but rather recording your findings in a 'what I saw when I went for a walk' way.

And remember, it's not necessarily about seeing an increasing amount of focus and clarity every single day. It's about noticing whatever is happening in the body and mind each time you sit down to meditate. Simply witnessing this transition, day after day, can in itself lead to a more relaxed way of seeing things, a greater willingness to accept and be part of change. We tend to identify very strongly with being a certain type of person, but when you do this exercise honestly, it makes you realise that actually we are much more than that one type of person. We're always changing, one moment to the next, one day to the next. And when you see this clearly, it becomes more difficult to hold on to any fixed views of how you see yourself. The result is a feeling of more freedom, of no longer needing to follow the same habitual patterns or cling to a certain identity.

Ten Suggestions for Living More Mindfully

It would be easy to dedicate an entire book to the ways in which you can best support your meditation practice, but I've suggested here what I consider to be just a few of the most important, in the hope that they'll help strengthen your practice of mindfulness in day-to-day life. Needless to say, the theme that runs throughout is one of awareness, an understanding of both oneself and others. It's about developing a gentle curiosity: watching, noticing and observing what's happening in every aspect of your life – how you act, how you speak, and how you think. But remember, it's not about trying to be someone else, it's about finding a sense of ease with you as you are, right now.

Perspective – choosing how you see your life

For meditation to be effective it doesn't really matter how you view your life. But it can be useful to acknowledge the general theme, because that way you can be more alert to the tendency to slip into negative patterns of thought. And it's this increased awareness that provides the potential for sustainable change.

It's also useful to notice how your perspective can shift – how one day you can get on a crowded train and not be too bothered about it, and yet on another occasion it appears to push every button you have. The good thing about this realisation is that clearly it's not what's happening *outside* of ourselves that causes us the most difficulty, but rather what's going on *inside* our own minds – which, thankfully, is something that can change. Noticing these shifting perspectives from day-to-day, and from moment to moment, can be a very strong support for your daily meditation.

Communication – relating to others

If you want to find a greater sense of happiness through the practice of meditation, taking out your frustrations on others is unlikely to encourage a calm and clear mind. Communicating skilfully and sensitively with other people is therefore essential on the road to getting some headspace. This could mean applying a greater sense of restraint, empathy or perspective to your relationships – or maybe all three!

That said, there are some people who, no matter how well intentioned *you* are, will still choose to pick a fight. In these situations there is often little you can do. Trying to empathise with them and recognise those similar states of mind within yourself can be helpful, but if someone is consistently unpleasant towards you, then it might be best to just stay well clear – if you possibly can that is.

Appreciation – smelling the roses

Have you ever noticed how much emphasis some people place on even the smallest amount of difficulty in their lives, and how *little* time they spend reflecting on moments of happiness? Part of the reason for this goes back to the idea that happiness is somehow 'rightfully ours', and that everything else is therefore wrong or out of place.

The idea of taking time out to be grateful may sound a little trite to some, but it's essential if we want to get some more headspace. It's very difficult to be caught up in lots of distracting thoughts when there is a strong sense of appreciation in your life. And by developing a more heartfelt appreciation of what *we* have, we also begin to see more clearly what's missing in the lives of others.

Kindness – towards both yourself and others

When you're kind to someone else it feels good. It's not rocket science. It feels good for you and it feels good for them. It makes for a very happy, peaceful mind. But whilst you're at it, how about showing yourself some of that kindness – especially in learning to be more mindful. We live in a world with such high expectations that we can often be critical of our own progress in learning something new.

Fortunately, meditation has a strange way of bringing out the kindness in people – and practising kindness in everyday life will simply feed back into your meditation. Kindness makes the mind softer, more malleable and easier to work with in your practice. It creates a mindset that is less judgmental and more accepting. Clearly this has profound implications for our relationships with others.

Compassion – in the shoes of others

Compassion is not something that we can 'do' or 'create', it already exists in each and every one of us. If you think back to the blue sky analogy, the same principle applies to compassion. In fact, you could say that the blue sky represents both awareness and compassion in equal measure.

Sometimes compassion will arise spontaneously, like the clouds parting to reveal the blue sky. At other times we might have to make a conscious effort, which is a bit more like *imagining* what the blue sky looks like, even when it's obscured by clouds. But the more you imagine this scenario, the more likely it is to happen naturally. Compassion is a lot like empathy really, putting ourselves in the shoes of another and experiencing a shared sense of understanding.

Balance – a sense of equanimity

Life is not unlike the sea, ebbing and flowing throughout our lives. Sure, sometimes it's calm and serene, but at other times the waves can be so big that they threaten to overwhelm us. These fluctuations are an inevitable part of life. But when you forget this simple fact, it's easy to get swept away by strong waves of difficult emotions.

By training the mind through meditation it's possible to develop a more balanced approach, so that you experience a greater sense of equanimity in life. This shouldn't be confused with a boring existence where you float along in life like some emotion-less grey blob. In fact it's quite the opposite. Having greater awareness of your emotions means that, if anything, your experience of them will be heightened. It's just that in being less caught up in them, you will no longer feel as though you're at their mercy.

Acceptance – resistance is futile

No matter how fortunate your circumstances, life can at times be both stressful and challenging. We often try to ignore this fact and therefore feel frustrated and disappointed when we don't get our own way. Much like compassion, it can be useful to think back to the blue sky analogy when you reflect on acceptance.

With that in mind, the journey to acceptance is about discovering what we need to let go of, rather than what we need to start doing.

By noticing moments of resistance throughout the day, you can start to become more aware of what prevents acceptance from *naturally* arising. This in turn will allow you to view the thoughts and feelings that arise during your meditation with a much greater sense of ease.

Composure – letting-go of impatience

For many people, life has now become so busy, so hectic, that a sense of impatience is perhaps inevitable. In these moments, you may notice your jaw tightening, your foot tapping, or your breath getting increasingly shallow. But by *noticing* the impatience with a genuine sense of curiosity, the very nature of it begins to change. Somehow the momentum slows down and its grip is released.

Impatience is just as likely to show up in your meditation practice as it is in everyday life – one simply reflecting the other. In fact, if you're like most people you may well find yourself asking, 'Why am I not experiencing results more quickly?' But remember, meditation is not really about achievement and results – which is why it's such a nice change of pace from the rest of life. Instead it's about learning to be aware, to rest in that space of natural awareness with a genuine sense of ease.

Dedication – sticking with it

Mindfulness is about a fundamental shift in the way you relate to your thoughts and feelings. While that may sound exciting, or perhaps a little overwhelming, it's done by repeating the exercise little and often. So this means practising meditation on a regular basis, no matter how you feel. Like any other skill, you'll become more confident and familiar with the feeling of mindfulness the more often you apply it.

By practising in this way – little and often – you can slowly start to build up a stable sense of awareness in your meditation, which will naturally feed through to the rest of your life. Likewise, by being more mindful in everyday life, it will have a positive impact on your practice. If you're really clear in your motivation, knowing why you're learning meditation and who those people are around you that are likely to benefit from your increased sense of head-space, then you're unlikely to have trouble sitting down for ten short minutes each day.

Presence – living life skilfully

Living skilfully can mean having the presence of mind to restrain yourself when you think you might say or do something you'll later regret. It can also mean having the strength and stability of awareness to respond sensitively to difficult situations rather than reacting impulsively. So living skilfully requires a certain amount of discriminating wisdom.

Unfortunately, wisdom can't be learnt from a book, no matter how profound the writing. Instead it relates to an *experiential* under-standing of life, which meditation can help to enhance. In the same way that compassion and acceptance are reminiscent of the blue sky analogy, so too is presence. Because wisdom isn't something you can 'do' or 'make happen' – it's there in all of us. By becoming more familiar with that space within ourselves and trusting our instinct more fully, we can then learn to *apply* this quality of discriminating wisdom in everyday life. In short, we can begin to live more skilfully in the world.

Tales from the Clinic

James, 40

James is married with three children. He's a successful businessman and, although he works hard, he enjoys a good lifestyle. So it might surprise you to learn that James came to the clinic because he was suffering from anxiety. It's easy to forget that what we see on the surface is often very different to what's going on inside.

James explained how much he worried. He would worry about his wife going off with someone else; about his children getting injured; he would worry about the health of his parents; about his business and the people working for him. And he would worry about himself too. In fact, he frequently visited the doctor and used the internet to try and determine what disease he might have at any given time.

He said people were always telling him how lucky he was, what an amazing life he had, so how could he explain that he was in a constant state of anxiety. Likewise, how could he explain that having everything so good only made him more nervous, because he had that much more to lose. He said that just thinking about the anxiety made him anxious. He would then start to feel guilty, as though he was stupid for feeling that way and would worry that he might be losing his mind.

The idea of meditation occurred to James after he saw something about it on television. He said that although it seemed a little 'out there', he was willing to give anything a go. Needless to say, he came to the clinic with many of the usual preconceptions about meditation, assuming that it was all about trying to stop thoughts and clear the mind of any unpleasant feelings. But he also came with an open mind and a willingness to embrace something new. In fact so much so that soon he was looking for any opportunity to apply the techniques. He applied mindfulness to his exercises at the gym, to eating his lunch, and even just sitting with the baby. He also quickly built up a daily practice of about twenty minutes.

Although enthusiasm doesn't always define the result, in James's case it seemed to make a big difference. Over time I watched as he became increasingly relaxed about the way he felt. We worked on a number of techniques, some of them generic and some specific to anxiety. Most of the focus was on how James *related* to his anxious thoughts. He had always seen them as a 'problem', something to 'get rid of' and he'd built up so much resistance to the thoughts, that he was battling them pretty much the entire day. It's a common reaction, but by resisting these feelings James was not only creating tension, but also exacerbating the situation by treating the thoughts as something tangible.

So it came as quite a surprise to James when I asked him to meditate less on the anxiety itself, which when left alone has a tendency to just come and go in its own time anyway, and instead focus on his *resistance* to the anxiety. After a little while he started to notice how his obsession with trying to control the anxiety was actually driving the anxiety itself. As he became increasingly aware of this tendency, so the situation started to unravel a little.

This didn't immediately stop the feeling of anxiety, but it did the change the way he related to it. Slowly, he gave up struggling to get rid of the thoughts and allowed the feelings of anxiety to flow a little more. During those few months I noticed that James started to find some humour in it all and not take himself or his thoughts too seriously. In fact he even started to share a few of these thoughts with other people. To his surprise his wife responded with relief, saying she'd always assumed that he was so 'sorted' and that she was the 'crazy' one. Knowing that he experienced these feelings too somehow took the pressure off a bit. He even made a couple of jokes about his anxiety with his friends in the pub.

I bumped into James recently. As expected, his enthusiasm for the meditation had kept him going and he was still sitting every morning. He said that although he still felt worried in certain situations, it didn't bother him in the same way. He no longer identified so strongly with the feeling of anxiety. Most importantly, he said he was no longer fearful of worry, which meant he didn't need to expend huge amounts of time and energy in trying to get rid of the feeling. The irony of it all, he said laughing, was that ever since he's stopped fighting the feeling, it didn't seem to come and visit quite so often.

Rachel, 29

Rachel came to the clinic because she had started having difficulty in sleeping. She'd seen her GP who had prescribed sleeping pills that Rachel was reluctant to take.

We discussed what might be causing the problem. Rachel thought it might be to do with being under a lot of pressure at work. She'd also moved in with her boyfriend and the fact she was working so much was causing arguments. He wasn't unsympathetic, but he felt she had her priorities wrong.

Rachel referred to her problem as 'insomnia'. I asked if she ever slept well and she said that sometimes she slept very well. This seemed to rule out insomnia, which tends to be both consistent and chronic. I asked if she could remember the first time it had happened. She said there'd been a particularly difficult day at work, about six months earlier, when she'd been preparing for an important presentation the next day and hadn't got home until midnight. By the time she got back her boyfriend was asleep, which she said made her feel guilty and a little lonely.

She said she remembered feeling very anxious as she lay in bed, with thoughts whizzing around in her mind. She was conscious of needing to look good the next day and to perform at her best, but the more she thought about it, the more wide awake she felt. In fact she found that the anxiety soon turned into frustration. First she got angry with her boss, then she got angry with her boyfriend, then she got angry with herself.

As it happens, the presentation went well the next day and the company won the contract, although Rachel said that she felt awful and didn't feel as though she'd contributed as well as she might have. What scared her the most, though, was that 'it' might happen again. By the time she got home she had already planned a strategy for getting to sleep. She was going to have a bath and go to bed very, very early. But even though she was tired, her body wasn't used to going to sleep that early, so again she lay awake for ages. She started to panic that 'it' was happening all over again and that she was in for another sleepless night. And so it went on. Of course, sometimes she would fall asleep straight away, but a pattern had developed where she was becoming increasingly anxious about not sleeping, which itself was causing her not to sleep.

After reassuring Rachel that sleeping difficulties are very common I introduced her to the basic approach to meditation and got her doing ten minutes every day. Although she thought it a bit strange that I was asking her to meditate in the morning when it was at night that she was having the problems, I explained that this wasn't necessarily how the mind worked and that it was more important that she had a stable daily practice.

I also asked her to look at her 'sleep hygiene'. This is how you prepare yourself for sleep. I asked her to make sure she only used the bedroom for sleep, as well as for being with her boyfriend of course. This helps strengthen the association between going to bed and going to sleep. I asked her to avoid taking naps during the day and explained how important it was to develop a regular time for sleep, going to bed and getting up at pretty much the same time each day – even at weekends to begin with. This may sound strict, but for the body and mind to learn new habits, they need to be repeated many times. I also asked her to avoid watching any stimulating television late at night, or playing computer games as both tend to leave the mind feeling a bit speedy. We discussed food too and the importance of eating at least a couple of hours before going to bed, allowing the body time to digest everything. Finally, we talked about the importance of buying an old-fashioned alarm clock, so that her mobile phone could live in another room overnight and she would not be tempted to look at e-mails.

In the first week Rachel got very excited as she'd slept well for a number of nights in a row. But the gremlins returned in the second week and she became impatient with her progress. We discussed the approach again and the attitude that needs to be applied in order to see the best results, and by the third week she was starting to see genuine progress.

We continued to meet for a couple of months, slowly working through the techniques until we reached those specific to sleeping (you can refer back to page 156). Now and then she would have a bad night, but by and large she was feeling more confident. Perhaps the biggest change was Rachel's perspective towards sleep. It no longer mattered that much. She said that looking back she couldn't understand how she'd taken it all so seriously. She said that she now recognises that her sleep won't always be perfect, but that's OK, she's happy to ride out the wave. And it's this change that has made it a truly sustainable approach.

Pam, 51

Pam was referred to the clinic by her doctor. She'd been on antidepressants for over three years and had tried various strategies to overcome the way she felt. She was still holding down a full-time job and, other than her GP and human resources manager at work, nobody knew about her depression. She described the depression as just 'sitting there', making everything look dark and pointless.

Pam had grown-up children who lived in other parts of the country and she had been divorced for ten years. Part of the reason for coming to see me was that she wanted to reduce her medication. With her doctor's support, she was planning to very slowly reduce the dosage. It was estimated this might take about a year. That may sound like a long time, but when people suddenly stop the long-term use of antidepressants, the results can be quite serious, so it's important to do it with your doctor's consent and in a very gentle way. The other advantage of this approach is that studies have consistently shown that relapse is far less likely if the withdrawal is gradual. Pam had read in the papers that meditation was supposed to be very good for treating depression, and was keen to give it a try.

At the heart of Pam's depression was the feeling that nothing went right for her and that everything was 'her fault'. In fact, it was remarkable the way in which she would reinforce these ideas. This sense of identity had become so strong that this was the only way she was able to see herself. But as long as she was continuing to engage with these thoughts, to nurture them even, there was little chance of her being free from the feeling of depression.

We spent a long time talking about how it was possible to step back from thoughts, to create a little more space. We talked about not needing to identify with the thoughts so much, that they were not who she was, but simply thoughts that had been coloured by the feelings of depression. And we talked about the analogy of the blue sky. When someone feels depressed, the idea that there is an underlying sense of happiness can seem laughable. The clouds have received so much attention and been given so much importance that they've become thick and dark in colour. For many people in this position it's difficult to remember a time when there might have been some blue sky, never mind the possibility of there actually being some now. But the analogy is important, because as long as you're searching for happiness or headspace outside of yourself, it will only ever lead to a temporary end to depression. What's more, it will intensify the feeling that what you're currently experiencing is somehow 'wrong'.

It wasn't an easy process for Pam but slowly the clouds did begin to part and she was reminded of what the blue sky felt like. The depression had become a strong habit so the clouds would return at first. But because it was a habit, it meant that it could be unlearned and the more Pam saw these patches of blue sky, the more she realised that the depression was not something permanent. She couldn't ignore these moments of calm and happiness that were creeping into her life, no matter how fleeting. At the same time, with the help of her doctor, she reduced her medication until she was ready to give it up altogether. At six months there'd been some reluctance to give up the medication. She felt it was part of who she was and worried who she was going to be if she was not that any more. In many ways it was about letting go of that identity. But by the time a year came around she was more than ready to stop. She added it felt a bit like saying goodbye to an old friend, but a friend she was very happy to see move on.

It was Pam's willingness to understand the feeling, and make friends with it, that ultimately enabled her to let go of it. What's more, she'd done it herself, taking time out each day to sit with her mind, no matter how she was feeling. Pam now keeps in touch by e-mail and is doing well. She still sometimes worries if she goes more than a few days or so feeling unhappy, fearing that the depression might be returning, but she says she's learnt that as long as she remains aware and remembers that they are just thoughts, she knows that she can never be harmed by them again.

Clare, 27

Sometimes people come to the clinic because they're looking to add something to their lives or improve a particular aspect. It might be a professional athlete looking for that competitive edge, or an artist or writer trying to access their creative potential. When Clare came to the clinic, it was with the intention of 'tapping into her creative reserves', as she liked to refer to it. She believed that creativity was something that was always there, but that she couldn't access it because of her busy mind. This view is not so different from the blue sky analogy; it's not that we need to 'create' creativity, but, rather, find a way to allow it to come to the surface.

Clare seemed to do a lot of different things. She composes music and plays an instrument, but writes too and has even published a book. She also paints, draws, and creates sculptures. She's an artist, in every sense of the word, and she's clearly good at what she does. But with so many different things going on at once she could never settle to one idea long enough for it to develop fully. As a result, her home and studio was full of half-finished verses, compositions and pieces of art.

Clare's biggest challenge, when practising the Take10 process, was noticing when the mind had drifted off – and it drifted off a lot. Clare would struggle simply to follow her breath up to a count of two or three. It's a little bit like links in a chain: a thought arises and if it's seen clearly, within the light of awareness, it doesn't have anywhere to go, it loses momentum and the focus remains with the object of meditation. But if that first thought appears so interesting that all awareness is lost, a second thought is created, and then a third and a fourth. It might be that there are so many links in the chain that five minutes will pass before you even notice that the mind has wandered off. But by repeating the exercise each day, the length of the chain gradually gets shorter. Your mind may still have a tendency to wander, but when it does, you'll see it happening a bit sooner and you can avoid getting caught up with the story.

Not only did Clare struggle with maintaining her focus, she also had difficulty remembering to take the ten minutes out of her day. She said that she really wanted to do it, but other things just seemed to get in the way. Some things do require urgent attention, but in most cases I'd guess that there's not much in life that can't wait for ten minutes. As a way of helping Clare, I suggested she put her meditation in her diary for each day. It was a simple way of saying 'this is just as important as any other part of your daily routine'. I also asked her to write down each time she was going to miss a session – just a short sentence to say why she wasn't going to do it. This isn't a retrospective to be done at the end of the day, it's about writing down, there and then, what it is you are about to do that can't wait ten minutes. Clare found this second exercise particularly useful. In fact, she said that any time she went to write an excuse in the book, it just looked so feeble that she went and did her ten minutes anyway.

I also asked Clare to choose a couple of activities in the day that she did on a regular basis, which she could use as further prompts to be mindful. For example, drinking a glass of juice in the morning, brushing her teeth, or preparing herself at her desk for work. The idea was not to do the activity while focusing on the breath, but rather using the activity as a support to be present and in the moment. If she was brushing her teeth then the focus was on the physical sensation of the toothbrush in the mouth, of the taste of the toothpaste, the smell of the toothpaste, and even the sound of the toothbrush moving backwards and forwards. And if the mind wandered off, in that moment she realised it had wandered, simply to return the focus to the physical senses. She enjoyed doing this and added a new activity each week. By the end of ten weeks, she had short bursts of mindfulness dotted throughout the day. The accumulative effect of this, together with the ten minutes of meditation each day, cannot be underestimated. For Clare, those moments were a time to 'regroup', to check whether she was spinning off into other ideas, and bring herself back to what she was working on at the time.

John, 45

John was at the clinic for one reason only: his wife had said that if he didn't do something to control his anger she was leaving. John did not have a physically violent relationship, with either his wife or his children, but there were elements of verbal aggression and bullying at home. In fact, John found himself getting irate with perfect strangers too. He would barge past people in shop queues, drive like a madman, and get upset when the smallest things didn't go his way. His blood pressure was high and he regularly felt a tightness in his chest.

John knew his behaviour was irrational, but said that it was as if a red mist would descend from nowhere. He had grown up in a household where emotions had neither been discussed nor expressed. He said that losing his job seemed to be the trigger for it all. It had put additional stress on the family, and John hated the fact he had nothing to do and that he'd seemingly lost his purpose in life.

I suggested that John gave the meditation two weeks and that if he'd not seen any benefit at all, then he would speak to his wife and discuss other options. I showed John how to do the ten minute exercise and spoke briefly about the kind of attitude that worked best.

When John came back to the clinic the following week, he said that far from calming him down, the meditation had actually made him more angry. He said that when he sat to do the exercise, all he could feel was anger, and that every single thought seemed to reflect that feeling. He felt angry at his old boss for making him redundant, but most of all he felt angry at himself. He was angry that he couldn't control the thoughts and that the thoughts resulted in him being unkind to the people he loved. Most of all he was angry that he wasn't the person he thought he was, or the person he wanted to be. I explained to John that the meditation would not have made things worse, but it may well have given him greater awareness and insight into just how angry he was feeling. But I also explained how reacting to the anger with more anger, while understandable and instinctive, was not the most helpful response.

I asked John how he reacted to his eldest daughter when she got angry. He said that in those situations, when she was really upset, all he wanted to do was put his arms around her. He said that if she let him he would just hold her. He knew from experience that there was nothing he could say that would make her feel better, it was just a case of being there to reassure her. I asked him to take a moment to think how it might feel if he approached his own anger in this way, to just allow it to be, without judgment or criticism. It was at this point that John started to cry. Although it was evidently uncomfortable and even embarrassing for him, it was quite uncontrollable. He said he hadn't realised how hard he was on himself, how he constantly beat himself up about the way he was feeling.

So John and I made a deal that his course of meditation wasn't going to be about getting rid of the anger, but instead meeting the anger with kindness and understanding. His task was to notice every time he got angry with himself, and in that moment of realising, rather than getting angry at himself for having got angry, to allow that feeling to have a bit of space. And if he felt himself spinning out of control, to remind himself how he would respond to that anger if it were his daughter's. John agreed to this, and he even started to sit and meditate twice a day while he was out of work. He said that he found the exercise challenging, and would often get caught up in the anger again, but said that when he remembered to remember, the feeling was as if everything suddenly became a bit softer.

We worked through a number of different techniques over the months, each specific to John's character, but that simple yet challenging task of meeting anger with kindness remained at the heart of them all. I'm happy to say that John is still very much together with his wife and he now has a job too. It's not that a miracle has occurred and that he never gets angry these days, but he says that life feels more comfortable now, and if he does get angry, he has a greater sense of perspective about it and is better able to deal with it.

Amy, 24

Amy is a single mum with a young daughter. She came to the clinic after speaking to her GP about various health concerns. She was underweight, had stopped menstruating, and was experiencing a small amount of hair loss. She was a determined woman, but seemed to carry the weight of the world on her shoulders. She'd struggled bringing up her daughter on her own and, although she was keen to be in a relationship, she didn't think anyone would really be interested in a single mum. Amy was intensely conscious of her body. She exercised at least once a day, ate a diet that was woefully inadequate, both in content and nutrition, and clearly had an unhealthy relationship with how she viewed herself.

I noticed Amy had sore-looking hands. I thought it might be eczema, but when I asked her she said that when she got stressed she had a tendency to wash her hands a lot and they got quite raw with the scrubbing. I asked her how often she did this. She said she would do it every time she touched something in public. She said that she knew it wasn't great, but that she only did it when she got stressed. She said the bigger problem was why her hair was falling out and why her periods had stopped so suddenly. So having agreed that she would also visit her GP, we agreed to meet once a week at the clinic.

In many ways, Amy's tendency to be very disciplined was useful when starting to meditate and she rarely missed a session. But sitting down to do it is one thing, applying the mind in the right way is quite another and Amy was heavily critical of herself and found it difficult to sit and observe her thoughts without passing judgment. She said most of the thoughts seemed to be about the exercise itself, almost as though there was a running commentary on how it was going. Amy had slipped into a pattern of thinking about thinking, which doesn't make for a very restful mind. She also seemed to be 'correcting' herself the whole time, trying to create the perfect state of mind she imagined meditation to be.

If you've never tried meditation before it may sound strange that people would still approach it in this way, despite being told that it's counterproductive. But habitual patterns of mind can be very strong and sometimes even though we're told to do things a different way, we just can't help ourselves. That's the interesting thing with meditation. It's a reflection of the way in which you relate to the world around you. So Amy's experience of meditation simply mirrored her attitude to life. Despite this approach, she still made some important insights into why she was living the way she was. She became more aware of her lack of self-worth and her tendency to compare herself physically to the young girls she taught at school, despite the fact that she was over ten years older. She also became more aware of the strong thought patterns that encouraged her to act in a way that was often obsessive in nature. We worked mostly with techniques that encouraged a sense of kindness and compassion towards herself. These techniques have the same essential elements of Take10 at their core, but are further developed to best suit the personality and character traits of the individual.

Amy has now been meditating for over three years. The insights that she had early on have continued to develop and she has made some remarkable changes to the way she feels about herself. She is still underweight, but no longer dangerously so. She still exercises every day, but says it's now more for enjoyment than punishment and her periods have started again. Amy says that while she recognises obvious changes such as living a more healthy lifestyle and having a more balanced outlook on life, it's actually the way she feels about herself that has changed the most. She says she feels as though she's found something within herself that reminds her that she's OK, no matter how she might feel on the outside – so that even when she slips back into old ways of thinking, she somehow feels OK with that.

Tom, 37

Tom came to the clinic describing himself as 'a professional addict'. Over the past fifteen years he had been addicted to alcohol, drugs, cigarettes, sex, gambling and food. Sometimes it was just the one addiction, and at other times it was several at once. He'd been in and out of rehab a few times, and when he came to the clinic he belonged to so many different support groups that he had just one night free each week to simply relax or meet up with what he called his 'non-addict' friends.

Now it's important to say that if you feel as though you or others are at risk as a result of your addictive behaviour you should always consult a doctor before following an approach such as mindfulness. Tom had seen his doctor on a number of occasions, but he felt as though he'd tried everything and yet was still falling back into the same old patterns of addictive behaviour.

Tom was single and had no children, although he said he

desperately wanted a family. This was complicated by the fact that he'd come to the conclusion he was probably gay. He'd been involved in various relationships over the years, but none had lasted – more often than not because of his insatiable appetite for something new. Tom was always chasing something, and as long as he was involved in doing something, he felt OK. But as soon as he stopped, he felt on edge. He had built up an array of distractions that he could dive into. There were those that were socially acceptable, such as eating and drinking, and then there were those that he hid.

Tom had been through so much therapy over the years that he had come to think he knew it all, and was no longer so receptive to new ideas. His feelings sounded as if they had been analysed, pulled apart and put back together in the form of a psychiatric evaluation. It's not just with therapy that this can happen. It can happen with meditation and mindfulness too, where the ideas are simply applied at an intellectual level, but don't actually become part of one's being. That said, it's much harder to do with meditation, because in the silence of sitting, there really is nowhere to hide. Some of the treatment he'd had was invaluable and the support groups continued to be a great source of comfort and security to him, but he felt let down by others.

This was a good opportunity for me to remind Tom that I couldn't promise him results, but I could tell him about the research being done into mindfulness and addiction, and I could speak from experience and tell him what other people had got out of the exercises. I explained that the success of the process would depend on his willingness to follow the programme, his discipline to do it each day, and a commitment to keeping an open mind. Tom agreed and left the clinic feeling very optimistic, having been led through the ten-minute exercise that was to be his homework for the week. To his surprise, he'd found it easier than he expected, which in turn gave him a huge amount of encouragement. Meditation can seem an alien concept for people who've not done it before, so it's understandable if they worry it's going to be impossible to do. But once you've actually tried it, and seen for yourself that you can do it, it's not such a big deal, it's just sitting down and taking ten minutes out to unwind, to appreciate the silence. Even if your mind is all over the place at first, being able to sit there for ten minutes gives you a belief and inner confidence that you can do it every time.

For Tom, this approach was very different to anything he'd tried in the past. He'd been used to having therapy every week for years, and he said that the 'work' was usually done during that session each week. Sometimes he would be given things to think about during the week, but mostly it was about turning up and talking through issues from childhood. He said he felt the responsibility for 'sorting him out' was very much with the therapist. With this in mind, I pointed out that I was not a therapist, and that the responsibility would be with him this time. This idea seemed to scare Tom a little, the implications being that if he was responsible, then he would also be to blame if it didn't go well. No matter how much I explained that there was no *blame* in meditation, he didn't seem convinced.

While it would be inappropriate to say that Tom became addicted to meditation, he went at it with an enthusiasm and discipline that I've rarely seen before. Had the dependency on a substance simply been replaced by a dependency on the feeling he experienced in meditation? Possibly, although it appeared to be much more than that. And besides, if he was going to be dependent on something in life, it's hard to imagine anything more beneficial than meditation. To tackle the issue of dependency, we also discussed the possibility of him coming every other week, rather than every week, and then just once a month. These were big steps for Tom. It meant him taking responsibility for the health of his own body and mind, rather than blaming someone else if it didn't go well. He still gets in touch if he hits a tricky spot or needs some guidance, but mostly he's content to sit with whatever it is and see how it plays out, in both his mind and his life. He still attends some of the support groups, but says he feels as though he can now be there to help support others, rather than going there just to be supported himself.

Offline Diary

Day 1

1 Did you make time to do Take10 today?   ○ Yes   ○ No

If you didn't manage it today, rather than give yourself a hard time about it, simply remind yourself how important it is to get some headspace and schedule it in your diary for tomorrow.

2 How did you feel immediately *before* Take10?

Did you feel comfortable with that feeling?   ○ Yes   ○ No

3 How did you feel immediately *after* Take10?

Did you feel comfortable with that feeling?   ○ Yes   ○ No

4 What was your mood today and how did it change throughout the day?

5 Were you aware of the little things as you went through the day?   ○ Yes   ○ No

Did you notice the warmth of the water in the shower this morning?   ○ Yes   ○ No

6 Did you notice anything today that you've never noticed before? If so, what?

Day 2

1 Did you make time to do Take10 today? ◯ Yes ◯ No

If you didn't manage it today, rather than give yourself a hard time about it, simply remind yourself how important it is to get some headspace and schedule it in your diary for tomorrow.

2 How did you feel immediately *before* Take10?

Did you feel comfortable with that feeling? ◯ Yes ◯ No

3 How did you feel immediately *after* Take10?

Did you feel comfortable with that feeling? ◯ Yes ◯ No

4 What was your mood today and how did it change throughout the day?

5 Were you aware of the little things as you went through the day? ◯ Yes ◯ No

Did you notice the taste and texture of your breakfast this morning? ◯ Yes ◯ No

6 Did you notice anything today that you've never noticed before? If so, what?

Day 3

1 Did you make time to do Take10 today? ⭘ Yes ⭘ No

If you didn't manage it today, rather than give yourself a hard time about it, simply remind yourself how important it is to get some headspace and schedule it in your diary for tomorrow.

2 How did you feel immediately *before* Take10?

Did you feel comfortable with that feeling? ⭘ Yes ⭘ No

3 How did you feel immediately *after* Take10?

Did you feel comfortable with that feeling? ⭘ Yes ⭘ No

4 What was your mood today and how did it change throughout the day?

5 Were you aware of the little things as you went through the day? ⭘ Yes ⭘ No

Did you notice the smell of toothpaste as you brushed your teeth? ⭘ Yes ⭘ No

6 Did you notice anything today that you've never noticed before? If so, what?

Day 4

1 Did you make time to do Take10 today? ○ Yes ○ No

If you didn't manage it today, rather than give yourself a hard time about it, simply remind yourself how important it is to get some headspace and schedule it in your diary for tomorrow.

2 How did you feel immediately *before* Take10?

Did you feel comfortable with that feeling? ○ Yes ○ No

3 How did you feel immediately *after* Take10?

Did you feel comfortable with that feeling? ○ Yes ○ No

4 What was your mood today and how did it change throughout the day?

5 Were you aware of the little things as you went through the day? ○ Yes ○ No

Did you notice the weight of the body pressing against the chair when you first sat down today? ○ Yes ○ No

6 Did you notice anything today that you've never noticed before? If so, what?

Day 5

1 Did you make time to do Take10 today? ◯ Yes ◯ No

If you didn't manage it today, rather than give yourself a hard time about it, simply remind yourself how important it is to get some headspace and schedule it in your diary for tomorrow.

2 How did you feel immediately *before* Take10?

Did you feel comfortable with that feeling? ◯ Yes ◯ No

3 How did you feel immediately *after* Take10?

Did you feel comfortable with that feeling? ◯ Yes ◯ No

4 What was your mood today and how did it change throughout the day?

5 Were you aware of the little things as you went through the day? ◯ Yes ◯ No

Did you notice the sensation of the breeze on your skin as you were walking outside today? ◯ Yes ◯ No

6 Did you notice anything today that you've never noticed before? If so, what?

Day 6

1 Did you make time to do Take10 today? ◯ Yes ◯ No

If you didn't manage it today, rather than give yourself a hard time about it, simply remind yourself how important it is to get some headspace and schedule it in your diary for tomorrow.

2 How did you feel immediately *before* Take10?

Did you feel comfortable with that feeling? ◯ Yes ◯ No

3 How did you feel immediately *after* Take10?

Did you feel comfortable with that feeling? ◯ Yes ◯ No

4 What was your mood today and how did it change throughout the day?

5 Were you aware of the little things as you went through the day? ◯ Yes ◯ No

Did you notice the sound of birds outside today? ◯ Yes ◯ No

6 Did you notice anything today that you've never noticed before? If so, what?

Day 7

1 Did you make time to do Take10 today? ◯ Yes ◯ No

If you didn't manage it today, rather than give yourself a
hard time about it, simply remind yourself how important
it is to get some headspace and schedule it in your diary
for tomorrow.

2 How did you feel immediately *before* Take10?

Did you feel comfortable with that feeling? ◯ Yes ◯ No

3 How did you feel immediately *after* Take10?

Did you feel comfortable with that feeling? ◯ Yes ◯ No

4 What was your mood today and how
did it change throughout the day?

5 Were you aware of the little things as
you went through the day? ◯ Yes ◯ No

Did you notice the smell of people's
perfume or aftershave today? ◯ Yes ◯ No

6 Did you notice anything today that
you've never noticed before? If so, what?

Day 8

1 Did you make time to do Take10 today? ◯ Yes ◯ No

If you didn't manage it today, rather than give yourself a
hard time about it, simply remind yourself how important
it is to get some headspace and schedule it in your diary
for tomorrow.

2 How did you feel immediately *before* Take10?

Did you feel comfortable with that feeling? ◯ Yes ◯ No

3 How did you feel immediately *after* Take10?

Did you feel comfortable with that feeling? ◯ Yes ◯ No

4 What was your mood today and how
did it change throughout the day?

5 Were you aware of the little things as
you went through the day? ◯ Yes ◯ No

Did you notice the taste of your tea,
coffee or drink this afternoon? ◯ Yes ◯ No

6 Did you notice anything today that
you've never noticed before? If so, what?

Day 9

1 Did you make time to do Take10 today? ◯ Yes ◯ No

If you didn't manage it today, rather than give yourself a hard time about it, simply remind yourself how important it is to get some headspace and schedule it in your diary for tomorrow.

2 How did you feel immediately *before* Take10?

Did you feel comfortable with that feeling? ◯ Yes ◯ No

3 How did you feel immediately *after* Take10?

Did you feel comfortable with that feeling? ◯ Yes ◯ No

4 What was your mood today and how did it change throughout the day?

5 Were you aware of the little things as you went through the day? ◯ Yes ◯ No

Did you notice the sensation of your feet against the floor when you were walking today? ◯ Yes ◯ No

6 Did you notice anything today that you've never noticed before? If so, what?

Day 10

1 Did you make time to do Take10 today? ◯ Yes ◯ No

If you didn't manage it today, rather than give yourself a hard time about it, simply remind yourself how important it is to get some headspace and schedule it in your diary for tomorrow.

2 How did you feel immediately *before* Take10?

Did you feel comfortable with that feeling? ◯ Yes ◯ No

3 How did you feel immediately *after* Take10?

Did you feel comfortable with that feeling? ◯ Yes ◯ No

4 What was your mood today and how did it change throughout the day?

5 Were you aware of the little things as you went through the day? ◯ Yes ◯ No

Did you notice the temperature of the different parts of the body today? ◯ Yes ◯ No

6 Did you notice anything today that you've never noticed before? If so, what?

Sources for Research Findings

The Approach

1 The Mental Health Foundation. (2010). *The Mindfulness Report*. London: The Mental Health Foundation. http://www.bemindful.co.uk/about_mindfulness/mindfulness_evidence#

2 Davidson, R. J., Kabat-Zinn, J., Schumacher, J., Rosenkranz, M., Muller, D., Santorelli, S. F., *et al.* (2003). 'Alterations in brain and immune function produced by mindfulness meditation'. *Psychosomatic Medicine*, 65(4), 564–570.

3 Lieberman, M. D., Eisenberger, N. I., Crockett, M. J., Tom, S. M., Pfeifer, J. H., & Way, B. M. (2007). 'Putting Feelings Into Words: Affect Labeling Disrupts Amygdala Activity in Response to Affective Stimuli'. [Article]. *Psychological Science*, 18(5), 421-428. doi: 10.1111/j.1467-9280.2007.01916.x

Creswell, J. D., Way, B. M., Eisenberger, N. I., & Lieberman, M. D. (2007). Neural correlates of dispositional mindfulness during affect labeling. *Psychosomatic Medicine*, 69(6), 560-565. doi: 10.1097/PSY.0b013e3180f6171f.

4   Benson H., Beary J. F., Carol M. P.: 'The relaxation response'. *Psychiatry*, 1974; 37: 37-45.
    Wallace R. K., Benson H., Wilson A. F: 'A wakeful hypometabolic state'. *Am J Physiol*, 1971; 221: 795-799
    Hoffman J. W., Benson H., Arns P. A. *et al*: 'Reduced sympathetic nervous system responsivity associated with the relaxation response'. *Science*, 1982; 215: 190-192.
    Peters R. K., Benson H., Peters J. M.: 'Daily relaxation response breaks in a working population: II. Effects on blood pressure'. *Am J Public Health*, 1977; 67: 954-959.
    Bleich H. L., Boro E. S.: 'Systemic hypertension and the relaxation response'. *N Engl J Med*, 1977; 296: 1152-1156.
    Benson H., Beary J. F., Carol M. P.: 'The relaxation response'. *Psychiatry*, 1974; 37: 37-45.
    Davidson, R. J., Kabat-Zinn, J., Schumacher, J., Rosenkranz, M., Muller, D., Santorelli, S. F., *et al.* (2003). 'Alterations in brain and immune function produced by mindfulness meditation'. *Psychosomatic Medicine*, 65(4), 564-570. doi: 10.1097/01.psy.0000077505.67574.e3.
5   Miller, John J., Ken Fletcher, and Jon Kabat-Zinn. 1995. 'Three-year follow-up and clinical implications of a mindfulness meditation-based stress reduction intervention in the treatment of anxiety disorders'. *General Hospital Psychiatry* 17, (3) (05): 192-200.
    Kabat-Zinn, J., Massion, A. O., Kristeller, J., Peterson, L. G., Fletcher, K., Pbert, L., *et al.* (1992). Effectiveness of a meditation-based stress reduction program in the treatment of anxiety disorders. *American Journal of Psychiatry*, 149, 936–943.

The Practice

1   Grant, J. A., Courtemanche, J., Duerden, E. G., Duncan, G. H., & Rainville, P. (2010). 'Cortical thickness and pain sensitivity in zen meditators'. *Emotion*, 10(1), 43-53. doi: 10.1037/a0018334.
2   Kuyken, W., Byford, S., Taylor, R. S., Watkins, E., Holden, E., White, K., et al. (2008). 'Mindfulness-based cognitive therapy to prevent relapse in recurrent depression'. *Journal of Consulting and Clinical Psychology*, 76(6), 966-978. doi: 10.1037/a0013786.
3   Kabat-Zinn, J., Wheeler, E., Light, T., Skillings, A., Scharf, M. J., Cropley,

T. G., et al. (1998). 'Influence of a mindfulness meditation-based stress reduction intervention on rates of skin clearing in patients with moderate to severe psoriasis undergoing phototherapy (UVB) and photo-chemotherapy (PUVA)'. *Psychosomatic Medicine*, 60(5), 625-632.

4 Hofmann, S. G., Sawyer, A. T., Witt, A. A., & Oh, D. (2010). 'The effect of mindfulness-based therapy on anxiety and depression: A meta-analytic review'. *Journal of Consulting and Clinical Psychology*, 78(2), 169-183. doi: 10.1037/a0018555.

5 Buck Louis, G. M., Lum, K. J., Sundaram, R., Chen, Z., Kim, S., Lynch, C. D., . . . Pyper, C. 'Stress reduces conception probabilities across the fertile window: evidence in support of relaxation'. *Fertility and Sterility*, In Press, Corrected Proof. doi: 10.1016/j.fertnstert.2010.06.078.

6 University of Oxford (2010, August 11). Study suggests high stress levels may delay women getting pregnant. Retrieved January 12, 2011, from http://www.ox.ac.uk/media/news_releases_for_journalists/100811. html.

The Integration

1 Kristeller, J. L., & Hallett, C. B. (1999). 'An Exploratory Study of a Meditation-based Intervention for Binge Eating Disorder'. *Journal of Health Psychology*, 4(3), 357-36.
Tang, Y. Y., Ma, Y., Fan, Y., Feng, H., Wang, J., Feng, S., . . . Fan, M. (2009). 'Central and autonomic nervous system interaction is altered by short-term meditation'. *Proceedings of the National Academy of Sciences of the United States of America*, 106(22), 8865-8870.
Tang, Y.-Y., Lu, Q., Geng, X., Stein, E. A., Yang, Y., & Posner, M. I. (2010). 'Short-term meditation induces white matter changes in the anterior cingulate'. *Proceedings of the National Academy of Sciences*, 107(35), 15649-15652.

2 University of Pennsylvania, (2010, February 12). Building Fit Minds Under Stress: Penn Neuroscientists Examine the Protective Effects of Mindfulness Training. Retrieved January 9, 2011, from http://www. upenn.edu/pennnews/news/building-fit-minds-under-stress-penn-neuroscientists-examine-protective-effects-mindfulness-tra.

3 Jacobs, G. D., Benson, H., & Friedman, R. (1996). 'Perceived Benefits in a Behavioral-Medicine Insomnia Program: A Clinical Report'. *The*

American Journal of Medicine, 100(2), 212-216. doi: 10.1016/s0002-9343(97)89461-2.

Ong, J. C., Shapiro, S. L., & Manber, R. (2008). 'Combining Mindfulness Meditation with Cognitive-Behavior Therapy for Insomnia: A Treatment Development Study'. *Behavior Therapy*, 39(2), 171-182. doi: 10.1016/j.beth.2007.07.002.

Ong, J. C., Shapiro, S. L., & Manber, R. (2009). 'Mindfulness Meditation and Cognitive Behavioral Therapy for Insomnia: A Naturalistic 12-Month Follow-up'. *EXPLORE: The Journal of Science and Healing*, 5(1), 30-36. doi: 10.1016/j.explore.2008.10.004.

4   Zeidan, F., Johnson, S. K., Diamond, B. J., David, Z., & Goolkasian, P. (2010). 'Mindfulness meditation improves cognition: Evidence of brief mental training'. *Consciousness and Cognition*, 19(2), 597-605. doi: 10.1016/j.concog.2010.03.014.

University of Carolina,(2010, April 16. Experiment Shows Brief Meditative Exercise Helps Cognition. Retrieved January 9, 2011, from http://www.publicrelations.uncc.edu/default.asp?id=15&objId=656.

5   Pagnoni, G., & Cekic, M. (2007). 'Age effects on gray matter volume and attentional performance in Zen meditation'. *Neurobiology of Aging*, 28(10), 1623-1627. doi: 10.1016/j.neurobiolaging.2007.06.008.

HEADspace

. . . .

**For information on
Headspace products and events,
or to find out more about the
Headspace Foundation,
please visit
www.getsomeheadspace.com**

. . . .